1 & 2 THESSALONIANS
THE 3:16 SERIES

UNQUENCHABLE
FAITH

DAVID FAUST

HEARTSPRING PUBLISHING · JOPLIN, MISSOURI

Copyright © 2004
HeartSpring Publishing
www.heartspringpublishing.com
A division of College Press Publishing Co.

Toll-free order line 800-289-3300
On the web at www.collegepress.com

The 3:16 Series (Colossians 3:16)
"Let the word of Christ dwell in you richly . . . ."

Cover design by Brett Lyerla
Interior design by Dan Rees

Library of Congress Cataloging-in-Publication Data

Faust, David.
    Unquenchable faith/ by David Faust.
        p. cm. — (3:16 series)
    ISBN 0-89900-492-X (pbk.)
    1. Bible. N.T. Thessalonians—Criticism, interpretation, etc.   2. Spiritual life—Biblical teaching.   I. Title.   II. Series.
    BS2725.52.F38 2004
    227'.81'0071—dc22

                                                              2004010981

HEARTSPRING'S 3:16 SERIES

The apostle Paul encouraged Christians in the first century and therefore us today to "**allow the Word of Christ to dwell in us richly**" (Colossians 3:16, *NIV*).

The 3:16 Series is based on this verse in Colossians. The series is designed primarily for small group study and interaction but will also prove fruitful for individual study. Each participant is encouraged to read the chapter before the group's meeting. The interaction questions are designed to be the focal point of your group's discussion time.

Psalm 119:11 says, "*I have hidden Your Word in my heart that I might not sin against You.*" One noteworthy feature of this series is that each study includes a suggested memory verse (a short verse or two from the passage that is being studied). A 5☐8-inch card has been inserted at the back of the book for you to take these verses with you wherever you go and refer to them throughout your day.

The HeartSpring Publishing website will continually be updated with small group ideas and tips to further enhance your study of each New Testament book in the 3:16 series. Be sure to log on to www.heartspringpublishing.com (College Press) frequently!

"**Let the Word of Christ . . . have the run of the house.
Give it plenty of room in your lives.**"
(Col. 3:16 *The Message*)

PREVIEWING OUR STUDY OF 1&2 THESSALONIANS

DAVID FAUST

Jesus said, "I've come to start a fire on this earth—how I wish it were blazing right now!" (Luke 12:49, *The Message*). When we become Christians, the Lord starts a fire burning in our hearts. He wants us to have an unquenchable passion for his Word and for his work, for his people and for his purpose. First Thessalonians 5:19 says, "Do not quench the Spirit" (New American Standard Bible [NASB]). Do not "put out the Spirit's fire" (New International Version [NIV]). Do not "suppress or subdue" the Spirit (Amplified).

"Unquenchable" refers to a warm fire or a bright light that can't be extinguished—a determined desire that cannot be subdued, overcome, or destroyed. Did you ever try to blow out one of those birthday candles that refuses to go out? In Sunday school children sing a little chorus that says, "This little light of mine, I'm gonna let it shine. Won't let Satan blow it out. I'm gonna let it shine." Our light for Christ needs to be unquenchable.

"Unquenchable" can also refer to a constant thirst. "As the deer pants for streams of water, so my soul pants for you, O God. My soul thirsts for God, for the living God" (Ps 42:1,2). Jesus said, "Blessed are those who hunger and thirst for righteousness, for they will be filled" (Matt 5:6). He told the woman at the well he could give her "living water" so she would never be thirsty again. God quenches our thirst—and yet, paradoxically, we can never get enough of his living water. Peter wrote, "Like newborn babies, crave pure spiritual milk, so that by it you may grow up in your salvation, now that you have tasted that the Lord is good" (1 Pet 2:2,3).

The deeper we drink of God's blessings, the more we will have an unquenchable desire to love him more and serve him more.

Fanning the Flame in Thessalonica

Acts chapter 17 tells how the apostle Paul and his coworker Silas planted a church in the Greek city of Thessalonica during their second missionary journey. "As his custom was, Paul went into the synagogue, and on three Sabbath days he reasoned with them from the Scriptures, explaining and proving that the Christ had to suffer and rise from the dead. 'This Jesus I am proclaiming to you is the Christ,' he said" (Acts 17:2,3).

An exciting new congregation was born, which included a wide variety of people. "Some of the Jews were persuaded and joined Paul and Silas, as did a large number of God-fearing Greeks and not a few prominent women" (Acts 17:4).

But as someone has said, "When God starts blessin', the devil starts messin'!" A group rose up in opposition to the Christians in Thessalonica. They formed a mob, started a riot, and dragged a Christian named Jason and some other believers before the city officials, shouting out accusations and stirring up the crowds. These Christians, they claimed, were "defying Caesar's decrees, saying that there is another king, one called Jesus." They said the followers of Jesus had "caused trouble all over the world" (Acts 17:5-9). The King James Version translates their words: "These that have turned the world upside down have come here also." From the world's perspective, they were turning the world upside down. But from God's perspective, they were turning it right side up!

Ever since the Garden of Eden, sin has turned things around. Instead of love, there's selfishness. Instead of peace, there's war. Instead of joy, there's frustration and disappointment. Instead of generosity, there's greed. Instead of life, there's death. The world is upside down, but Jesus came to turn it right side up. And ever since the first century he's been calling his church to help turn things around.

Paul didn't spend a lot of time in Thessalonica, but the church thrived there and became a model congregation (1 Thess 1:7). Around A.D. 50, Paul wrote two letters to encourage the believers to live holy lives in the midst of a culture that was hostile to their Christian values. First and Second Thessalonians are two of Paul's earliest letters included in the New Testament. They deal with practical issues like how to remain sexually pure, how to earn the respect of others, and how to handle ourselves in the workplace. They also have a lot to say about Jesus' second coming. (Every chapter of 1 Thessalonians ends with a reference to the return of Christ.)

Fanning the Flame in Our Lives Today

The goal of this book is to help you and your group fan into flame your passion for God by learning and applying the powerful lessons found in 1 and 2 Thessalonians.

Chapter One: Unquenchable! (1 Thessalonians 1:1-3)

This chapter introduces our study by explaining the importance of holy zeal in a Christian's life. We'll evaluate what we're passionate about and consider some biblical examples of people who had an unquenchable love for God. What happens when we fan into flame our passion for God? We develop an unquenchable faith, hope, and love.

Chapter Two: An Unquenchable Love for Lost People (1 Thessalonians 1:4-10)

The Thessalonian church was so filled with zeal for God's good news, Paul says the message "rang out" from them and their faith in God became known everywhere (1 Thess 1:8). This chapter will help us learn how we can "ring out the good news" to our families, friends, and neighbors.

Chapter Three: An Unquenchable Desire to Be a Godly Leader (1 Thessalonians 2:1-12)

If you influence even one other person, you're a leader. In 1 Thessalonians chapter 2, the apostle Paul describes his own approach to leadership. In this chapter we will examine six marks of a godly leader that can help us grow in our own leadership roles.

Chapter Four: An Unquenchable Devotion to God's Word (1 Thessalonians 2:13)

The apostle Paul makes it clear that his teachings and writings are not merely "the word of men," but "the word of God, which is at work in you who believe" (1 Thess 2:13). What evidence supports this claim? Why do we believe the Bible is inspired by God? This chapter will lead us to examine why we believe the Bible is true, and will challenge us not only to believe it but also to live it.

Chapter Five: An Unquenchable Desire to Build Up the Church (1 Thessalonians 2:14–3:13)

Many people today don't like the church very well. Why should we love the church? What benefits will we receive when we become actively involved in the fellowship of believers? This chapter takes a realistic look at what it means to belong to the body of Christ.

Previewing Our Study of 1 & 2 Thessalonians

Chapter Six: An Unquenchable Commitment to Sexual Purity
(1 Thessalonians 4:1-12)

Sex is like a fire. Keep it inside the fireplace, and it warms your house. Let it rage out of control, and people get hurt. The apostle Paul provides clear guidance about sexual morality. This chapter not only takes an honest look at the consequences of sexual sin, but also discusses the positive side of sexual purity.

Chapter Seven: Unquenchable Hope for the Future
(1 Thessalonians 4:13-18)

Hope is one of the greatest needs of the human heart. Fortunately, it is also one of the main themes of the Christian gospel. This chapter examines a teaching at the very heart of 1 and 2 Thessalonians: the glorious return of Jesus Christ and the hope he provides as we face the reality of death.

Chapter Eight: An Unquenchable Passion for Changing Our Culture
(1 Thessalonians 5:1-8)

What does it mean to be "children of light" in a dark world? This chapter discusses how Christians should deal with our culture. It presents four practical steps we can take if we want to make a positive difference for the Lord's sake.

Chapter Nine: Unquenchable Encouragement
(1 Thessalonians 5:9-28)

First Thessalonians 5:11 says, "Therefore encourage one another and build each other up, just as in fact you are doing." In a world that tears people down, we are God's construction crew. This chapter opens our eyes to others who need our encouragement and offers some practical ways we can put encouragement into practice.

Chapter Ten: An Unquenchable Determination to Persevere
(2 Thessalonians 1:1-12)

How can we develop spiritual staying power? The Bible says that the testing of our faith develops perseverance (James 1:3). This chapter encourages us to live for the glory of God over the long haul—even when hardships test our faith.

Chapter Eleven: An Unquenchable Love for the Truth
(2 Thessalonians 2:1-17; 3:1-5)

In today's world, truth is a pearl of great price. Second Thessalonians chapter two warns about the deceptiveness of Satan. How can we

Previewing Our Study of 1 & 2 Thessalonians

recognize the counterfeit and hold onto the genuine? This chapter will help us analyze and apply a very challenging section of God's Word so that we can develop a deeper and more confident love for the truth.

Chapter Twelve: An Unquenchable Commitment to God's Work (2 Thessalonians 3:6-18)

The Bible has a lot to say about how we should conduct ourselves in our daily work. In a Greek culture that looked down on manual labor, some members of the Thessalonian church had become lazy and idle. Paul challenged them to see that a healthy work ethic is a noble and necessary part of the Christian life. This closing chapter will help us examine how we are demonstrating our faith in the workplace.

TABLE OF CONTENTS

UNQUENCHABLE
FAITH

Chapter	Title	1 Thessalonians Text	Page
One	UNQUENCHABLE	1:1-3	11
Two	AN UNQUENCHABLE LOVE FOR LOST PEOPLE	1:4-10	22
Three	AN UNQUENCHABLE DESIRE TO BE A GODLY LEADER	2:1-12	34
Four	AN UNQUENCHABLE DEVOTION TO GOD'S WORD	2:13	46
Five	AN UNQUENCHABLE DESIRE TO BUILD UP THE CHURCH	2:14–3:13	58
Six	AN UNQUENCHABLE COMMITMENT TO SEXUAL PURITY	4:1-12	68
Seven	UNQUENCHABLE HOPE FOR THE FUTURE	4:13-18	79
Eight	AN UNQUENCHABLE PASSION FOR CHANGING OUR CULTURE	5:1-8	88
Nine	UNQUENCHABLE ENCOURAGEMENT	5:9-28	100

Chapter	Title	2 Thessalonians Text	Page
Ten	AN UNQUENCHABLE DETERMINATION TO PERSEVERE	1:1-12	111
Eleven	AN UNQUENCHABLE LOVE FOR THE TRUTH	2:1-17; 3:1-5	120
Twelve	AN UNQUENCHABLE COMMITMENT TO GOD'S WORK	3:6-18	128

10
‡
T
A
B
L
E

O
F

C
O
N
T
E
N
T
S

Unquenchable Faith

CHAPTER ONE

UNQUENCHABLE!

1 THESSALONIANS 1:1-3

My wife Candy and I enjoy hiking in the mountains. When we traveled to Bar Harbor, Maine, I was excited about hiking at nearby Acadia National Park, so I stopped at a gift shop in town and bought a little guidebook called *Best Easy Day Hikes*.

I would like to go on record as saying that the title of that book is a lie! The hikes could be done in a day, but most of them were definitely not *easy*. Evidently the book was written by someone who's in a lot better shape than we are. We quickly learned that if the book categorized a trail as "easy," for us the trail was actually going to be "challenging." If the book said a trail was going to be "moderate," for us the trail would be "hard." And if the book said a trail was "difficult," we'd better plan on driving our car.

But what really struck me was the opening chapter, called "Zero Impact," where the book warned hikers not to interfere with nature in any way: Don't pick wildflowers, don't feed the animals, don't leave the trails. The chapter summed up its advice in three "zero-impact principles": (1) "Leave with everything you brought." (2) "Leave no sign of your visit." (3) "Leave the landscape as you found it."[1]

Those may be good principles for preserving the environment, but they are a terrible way to live your life.

"Leave with everything you brought"? No! Job was right: "Naked I came from my mother's womb, and naked I will depart" (Job 1:21). You can't take worldly things with you when you die.

"Leave no sign of your visit"? No! The Lord wants us to make our own unique contributions and leave a mark on the world.

"Leave the landscape as you found it"? No! We're all here to make a difference—to change our culture's spiritual landscape and make it better.

How Much Zeal Do You Have?

When Dwight L. Moody was a young boy, he sat in the balcony listening when a little-known preacher named Henry Varley said, "The world has yet to see what God can do with a man who is fully yielded to him."

Moody said, "By the grace of God, I'll be that man."

How many people do you know who have that kind of passion for God? When Dave Thomas started the Wendy's franchise, he insisted on making the hamburgers square to show his restaurant wasn't going to "cut corners." But today, everyone seems to be cutting corners. When I was a college professor, students would ask, "How long does this term paper have to be?" What they really meant was, "How short can I get by with?"

Jesus said the greatest commandment is to "love the Lord your God with all your heart and with all your soul and with all your mind and with all your strength" (Mark 12:30). He told one group of corner-cutting Christians that he found their halfheartedness nauseating. "Because you are lukewarm—neither hot nor cold—I am about to spit you out of my mouth" (Rev 3:16).

What fires you up? What do you feel passionate about? What do you believe in so deeply that nothing could change your mind? What motivates you to do your best and give your all? The Bible calls this "zeal"—a wholehearted, passionate commitment to a great cause. Zeal is more than an emotional high or a fleeting moment of courage. It's a deep, determined desire to make your life count for something eternally worthwhile.

> What do you believe in so deeply that nothing could change your mind?

Ralph Waldo Emerson said, "Nothing great was ever achieved without enthusiasm." Martin Luther passionately desired to reform the church. Abraham Lincoln was gripped by a compelling burden to free the slaves and preserve the Union. Daniel Boone was determined to blaze a trail across the American frontier. Susan B. Anthony had a burning desire to ensure women had the right to vote. Martin Luther King had an unquenchable determination to advance the cause of civil rights.

In 1900 Wilbur Wright wrote a letter to a friend and said, "For some years I have been afflicted with the belief that flight is possible to man." His zeal was so great, he said, "I feel that it will soon cost me an increased amount of money if not my life." Neither Wilbur Wright nor his brother Orville ever graduated from high school, but they studied hard and passionately pursued their dreams. They didn't have a pilot's license, and no one had ever done it before, but they accomplished their goal. Today we can fly nearly anywhere in the world because the Wright brothers dared to pursue their dream.

Zeal is especially important for a follower of Christ.

Zeal is especially important for a follower of Christ. After Jesus drove the merchants and moneychangers out of the temple, his disciples remembered the prophecy that said, "Zeal for your house will consume me" (John 2:17, quoted from Ps 69:9). Jesus was consumed by zeal for the house of God. In fact, Jesus redefined "passion." Look up the word "passion" in the dictionary, and you will find the name of Christ mentioned there. "Passion" is from a Latin word for suffering. A "passion play" is a dramatic portrayal of the final hours leading up to Jesus' death on the cross. God didn't cut corners on the cross. In Gethsemane, when Jesus prayed, "Father, not my will but yours be done," it wasn't a new prayer. It was the way he lived his life. He was filled with a zealous determination to do the Father's will.

The apostle Paul was filled with passion for God. In Acts 20:24 he said, "I consider my life worth nothing to me, if only I may finish the race and complete the task the Lord Jesus has given me—the task of testifying to the gospel of God's grace." In Romans 12:11 he instructed Christians to "never be lacking in zeal, but keep your spiritual fervor, serving the Lord."

Dave Stone preaches to thousands at Southeast Christian Church in Louisville, Kentucky, but he always takes notes when he listens to other people preach. He's already an excellent speaker. Why take notes when someone else speaks? Because Dave has a passion for God and an unquenchable desire to keep improving as a communicator.

Prior to his death at the age of 98 in May 2003, Orrin Root wrote a weekly Bible commentary column for *The Lookout* magazine every week for 53 consecutive years. Why keep going so long? Mr. Root had an unquenchable desire to serve the Lord.

Unquenchable! 1

Who Cares?

A passionate love for God is completely countercultural. In today's world, most people drift toward one of two extremes: some care deeply about nothing, and others care deeply about the wrong things.

When Zeal Is Missing

Instead of being "zealous," many today are "zeal-less," apathetic, and cynical. Their attitude is captured by one word: "Whatever!" You disagree with the Bible and want to make up your own religious rules? "Whatever!" You're sleeping with a partner you haven't married? "Whatever!"

The "whatever" attitude even plagues churches. Sometimes a spiritual dullness sets in, like the way you feel when you eat too much Thanksgiving dinner—sluggish and overstuffed. What a disaster, when Christians have little passion for Christ and his work! The Lord wants us to be a lean, mean, disciple-making machine, not a lifeless organization going through the motions of religion.

It's even more tragic to find the "whatever" attitude among church leaders. Brennan Manning wrote, "Leadership in the church is not entrusted to successful fund-raisers, brilliant biblical scholars, administrative geniuses, or spellbinding preachers . . . but to those who have been laid waste by a consuming passion for Christ—passionate men and women for whom privilege and power are trivial compared to knowing and loving Jesus."[2]

The Bible describes a different kind of "whatever attitude" which requires an all-out commitment to God. "Whatever you do, whether in word or deed, do it all in the name of the Lord Jesus" (Col 3:17). "Whether you eat or drink or whatever you do, do it all for the glory of God" (1 Cor 10:31). "Whatever is true, whatever is noble, whatever is right, whatever is pure . . . lovely . . . admirable . . . excellent . . . praiseworthy—think about such things" (Phil 4:8).

When Zeal Is Misguided

The problem with others is not that they care about *nothing*, but that they care deeply about the *wrong* things or about things that are relatively unimportant. They crowd into a stadium to cheer their favorite team, but won't go to church to praise their heavenly Father. They rally to save the whales, but voice no protest when abortion kills a million babies a year. They rearrange their schedules to watch their favorite TV shows, but not to spend a few minutes in prayer. G.K. Chesterton said, "A puritan is a person who pours righteous indignation into the wrong things." Proverbs 19:2 says, "It is not good to have zeal without knowledge, nor to be hasty and miss the way."

It's not enough to be zealous. We need to be zealous for the right things! The apostle Paul was concerned about some Jewish leaders who were "zealous for God, but their zeal [was] not based on knowledge" (Rom 10:2). During Jesus' ministry, a group of social rebels called the Zealots tried to pressure Jesus into becoming a political king instead of a spiritual leader. Their zeal was misguided.

> **It's not enough to be zealous.**
> **We need to be zealous for the right things!**

Misguided zeal motivated Muslim zealots to fly airplanes into the World Trade Center. Misguided zeal makes Christians quarrel and divide over differing opinions about details of the Lord's return. I've seen Bible college students go to school as freshmen, excited and ready to turn the world right side up for Christ. Then by the time they graduate, they've lost their passion for the Lord—or worse, they have become experts at quarreling over issues that don't really build up the church or draw people closer to God. If churches and parachurch organizations don't equip and motivate our members to serve the Lord with wholehearted passion, something has gone seriously awry.

We need to pray the **Prayer for Proper Passion**:

"God, let me know what's really important in your eyes. Make me care deeply about those things. And let me refuse to worry about anything else."

King David said, "Bless the Lord, O my soul; And all that is within me, bless His holy name" (Ps 103:1, NASB). *"All that is within me"?* That's zeal! Acts 13:36 describes the death of David by saying, "For when David had served God's purpose in his own generation, he fell asleep." I want to serve God's purpose in my generation before I die—don't you?

SOME THINGS I CARE DEEPLY ABOUT

- I care deeply about worshiping God and praising him with all my heart.
- I care deeply about faithfulness to the Word of God—not a legalistic, pharisaical approach that turns Scripture into a lifeless book of rules, but a spirit of humble, loving obedience that thanks God for his truth and seeks to honor it in word and deed.

- I care deeply about communicating God's Word with clarity, enthusiasm, sincerity, and relevance.
- I care deeply about fairness and treating others with respect. God does not play favorites. If we disrespect people based on social, racial, or economic distinctions, it arouses God's righteous anger.
- I care deeply about my family—my wife, children, and grandchildren—and about helping others develop strong families too.
- I care deeply about Christian unity, and I'm dismayed when churches split over personality clashes and denominational politics.
- I care deeply about helping Christians know what we believe and why. I don't have much interest in theological speculations that only lead to confusion, frustration, and division.
- I care deeply that we should be people of integrity who keep our word, honor our promises, and prayerfully rely on God's power instead of our own.
- I care deeply about the principles of the Restoration Movement. I believe in the ideals expressed in slogans like these: "In faith, unity; in opinions, liberty; and in all things, love." "We aren't the only Christians, but we are Christians only." "Where the Bible speaks, we speak; where the Bible is silent, we are silent."
- I care deeply about helping unreached people come to Christ. I believe the Lord wants his church to be focused on reaching the lost—not preoccupied by trivial matters that detour and distract us from evangelism and discipleship.

Unquenchable Passion for God

In his first letter to the Christians who lived in a city called Thessalonica in first-century Greece, Paul recalled the Thessalonians' passionate zeal for the Lord. He wrote:

> Paul, Silas, and Timothy, to the church of the Thessalonians in God the Father and the Lord Jesus Christ: Grace and peace to you. We always thank God for all of you, mentioning you in our prayers. We continually remember before our God and Father your work produced by faith, your labor prompted by love, and your endurance inspired by hope in our Lord Jesus Christ (1 Thess 1:1-3).[3]

This text points out three results of an unquenchable passion for God in our lives: work produced by faith, labor prompted by love, and endurance inspired by hope.

Unquenchable Faith

First Paul mentions the "work produced by faith." If you enjoy gardening, you know it's hard work to plant tomatoes and then weed and water them all summer. But it's work produced by faith! You believe that when you bite into a juicy, delicious tomato in August, your work will be rewarded. It takes a lot of practice and self-discipline to sing with excellence or to play basketball well, but the satisfaction of a stellar musical performance or playing on a winning team makes the work worthwhile. If a student is interested in the subject of a class, it's less of a chore to read a book or listen to the professor's lecture. The "work produced by faith" may be hard at the moment, but it's ultimately satisfying and worthwhile.

> The "work produced by faith" may be hard at the moment, but it's ultimately satisfying and worthwhile.

Faith moves us to take risks we otherwise might avoid. A friend of mine is serving the Lord on a mission field in India where it's dangerous to be identified as a Christian. He risks his life for the sake of the gospel. His unquenchable faith takes him far outside his comfort zone instead of playing it safe. As someone has said, "A ship is safe in the harbor, but that's not what a ship is for."

Faith moves us to trust God for results we may not see for years to come. The Honor Roll of Faith in Hebrews chapter 11 lists one godly man and woman after another who lived by faith, but then notes, "These were all commended for their faith, yet none of them received what had been promised" (Heb 11:39). Their "work produced by faith" laid the groundwork for future generations to be blessed. An old proverb says, "One generation plants the tree, the next enjoys its shade."

Faith allows us to tap into the infinite power of God. God's work, not our own, produces the most fruit. Jesus said, "Apart from me, you can do nothing" (John 15:5).

Unquenchable Love

The apostle Paul also commends the Thessalonian Christians for their "labor prompted by love."

The phrase "labor of love" refers to hard, strenuous labor. Combing a toddler's hair—that's a pleasant job. Changing his diaper—that's a labor of love. Eating a nice meal—that's easy. Spending hours cooking it and then cleaning up the mess afterward—that's a labor of love.

A labor of love makes you sweat. It's the kind of work you do because you believe in it, even though it takes a sacrifice. It's a job that has to be done even when it's not fun, even when it brings no recognition or outward reward. Did Christ touch and heal lepers because it was fun? No, it was a labor of love. Was it easy for him to go to the cross? No, it was a labor of love, motivated by his unquenchable passion for the Father's will.

> A labor of love makes you sweat. It's the kind of work you do because you believe in it, though it takes a sacrifice.

As a student at Cincinnati Bible Seminary in the 1930s John Wilson would take a boat across the Ohio River each week so he could preach at a church in Kentucky. After he graduated, he would take a boat back across the river one day a week so he could continue his studies in graduate school to help him become a more effective preacher. Then after becoming senior minister at First Christian Church in Springfield, Ohio, for many years John made the 75-minute drive back to Cincinnati one day a week to teach a class in personal evangelism and help young ministers learn how to reach the lost. It was a labor of love.

Do you know someone who takes care of a loved one who has Alzheimer's disease? Someone who has served as a Sunday school teacher for many years? Someone who's always there when others are in need? They understand what it means to do a labor of love.

Unquenchable Hope

Finally, Paul reminds the Thessalonian believers about their "endurance (or steadfastness) inspired by hope."

For eight years, from 1965 to 1973, Admiral Jim Stockdale was a prisoner of war in Vietnam. He was tortured repeatedly during this period and lived in what the soldiers nicknamed the "Hanoi Hilton" with no rights as a prisoner, no time set for his release, and no certainty about whether he would survive to see his family again. As the highest-ranking officer in the prison, he felt the burden of leadership and he did everything he could to help the other prisoners survive without breaking down under the stress.

Once he beat himself with a stool and cut himself with a razor, deliberately disfiguring himself, so that his captors couldn't put him on videotape and use him as an example of a "well-treated prisoner." He set up rules to help his men deal with torture, and an elaborate communications system that used a series of tapping sounds so his men wouldn't feel so isolated.

Upon his release, Stockdale was awarded the Congressional Medal of Honor. When asked how he explained his perseverance, he said, "I never lost faith in the end of the story. I never doubted, not only that I would get out, but also that I would prevail in the end and turn the experience into the defining event of my life. . . ."[4] He was sustained by unquenchable hope.

But notice, the apostle Paul is talking about a specific kind of hope in 1 Thessalonians 1:3—"hope in our Lord Jesus Christ." As the songwriter put it, "My hope is built on nothing less than Jesus' blood and right-eousness." Alexander Maclaren wrote, "I remember once walking in the long galleries of the Vatican, on the one side of which there are Christian inscriptions from the catacombs, and on the other heathen inscriptions from the tombs. One side is all dreamy and hopeless; one long sigh echo-ing along the line of white marbles—'*Vale! Vale! In aeternum vale!*' (Farewell, farewell, forever farewell.) On the other side—'*In Christo, in pace, in spe.*' (In Christ, in peace, in hope.)"[5] The risen Christ makes all the difference. His resurrection gives us "living hope" (1 Peter 1:3).

> **Paul is talking about a specific kind of hope—
> "hope in our Lord Jesus Christ."**

Steve Skaggs and his family serve as missionaries in Botswana, Africa. Most of Botswana lies in the desert and is quite dry. Rain is scarce, but when it comes, it makes the desert come alive. Water means so much to the people there that their word for "rain" is the same word they use for "money." When Steve goes to the store, he spends "rain" (*pulas*). When a speaker addresses a crowd and the audience agrees with his words, they shout out, "*Pula!* (Rain)!"

One Christmas Steve and his family attended a concert featuring a 150-voice choir from Botswana, plus other choirs from as far away as Asia and America. Each group sang selections from Handel's *Messiah*. At the end, all the choirs joined together and sang "The Hallelujah Chorus." The crowd, including the president of Botswana, stood and applauded wildly.

The man next to Steve shouted out, "Pula!" And Steve says he thought, "Indeed. The message of Christ powerfully and beautifully deliv-ered. You're absolutely right, my friend. That's rain if I've ever felt it!"

May God open the floodgates of heaven and flood us with passion for serving him. Let it rain, brothers and sisters. Let it rain!

---

[1] Dolores Kong and Dan Ring, *Best Easy Day Hikes: Acadia National Park* (Guilford, CT: Falcon, 2001) 4, 5.

[2] Brennan Manning, *Abba's Child* (Colorado Springs: NavPress, 1994) 129.

[3] In a famous chapter about love, the apostle Paul wrote, "Now these three remain: faith, hope, and love—but the greatest of these is love" (1 Cor 13:13). Here in 1 Thessalonians 1:3, Paul again mentions faith, hope, and love, except this time he changes the order to faith, love, and hope.

[4] Jim Collins, *Good to Great* (New York: HarperCollins, 2001) 83-87.

[5] Alexander MacLaren, *Expositions of Holy Scripture*, Vol. 9 (Grand Rapids: Eerdmans, 1959) 246.

20

✝

C
H
A
P
T
E
R

1   *Unquenchable!*

Developing Unquenchable Faith

1. List three of your "passions"—things you care deeply about.

2. Would those who know you well say that you have a lot of zeal for the Lord? Why, or why not?

3. Do you agree that Christians should be zealous for our faith? What is the difference between healthy zeal and unhealthy fanaticism?

4. Do you ever cut corners in your relationship with God? What are some symptoms of lukewarmness in a Christian's life? How can such halfheartedness be prevented?

5. Tell the group about a time in your life when you have experienced one of the following:
   Work produced by faith,
   Labor prompted by love,
   Endurance inspired by hope.

6. Pray together for God to fan into flame your passion for him. Ask the Lord to use your study of 1 and 2 Thessalonians to help you grow in faith and obedience.

 Memory Verse 1 Thess 1:3 *We continually remember before our God and Father your work produced by faith, your labor prompted by love, and your endurance inspired by hope in our Lord Jesus Christ.*

CHAPTER TWO

AN UNQUENCHABLE
LOVE FOR LOST PEOPLE

1 THESSALONIANS 1:4-10

Dolly the cloned sheep died in February, 2003. She only lived to be six years old, about half as long as most sheep live. Dolly's birth was big news—a scientific breakthrough. While the future of flocks may be forever altered because of this discovery, the method of multiplication used in God's flock has not changed. You can't clone God's sheep. There's no quick, magic process for bringing a lost sheep back into God's fold. It usually takes a lot of time, effort, love, and patience.

There is no greater joy in life than to play a part in leading someone closer to Jesus. To take their hand and hear them say they believe Jesus is the Christ, the Son of God. To stand in the water and baptize them, and see the joy in their eyes as they begin a new life in Christ. But you won't experience that unless you get involved in the lives of people who do not share your Christian worldview.

If anyone ever had an unquenchable love for the lost, it was Jesus. He came seeking the broken, the sinful, the overlooked. He didn't just hang out with the sanitized safe crowd, but with eyebrow-raising associates like Zacchaeus and Mary Magdalene. Although he was sinless, sinners knew him as their friend.

> If anyone ever had an unquenchable love for the lost,
> it was Jesus.

Ringing Out the Message

The Thessalonian church had an unquenchable love for lost people. The apostle Paul told them, "Brothers loved by God, we know that he has chosen you, because our gospel came to you not simply with words, but also with power, with the Holy Spirit and with deep conviction. You know how we lived among you for your sake" (1 Thess 1:4,5).

Notice:

- There is life-changing power in the Word of God.
- The Holy Spirit works through the Word, which is the "sword of the Spirit" (Eph 6:17).
- The gospel produces deep conviction in our hearts—moving us to do what pleases the Lord.

Paul gave the Thessalonian believers a compliment when he told them, "You became imitators of us and of the Lord; in spite of severe suffering, you welcomed the message with the joy given by the Holy Spirit. And so you became a model to all the believers in Macedonia and Achaia" (1 Thess 1:6, 7).

The truth is so important that it should be welcomed "in spite of severe suffering." One reason Paul described the Thessalonian believers as a model church was their willingness to share their faith with others. Paul says, "The Lord's message rang out from you not only in Macedonia and Achaia—your faith in God has become known everywhere" (v. 8).

Some things are bad when they "ring out." When a cell phone rings during a worship service at church, that's annoying. When your alarm clock rings early in the morning, it's not a pleasant sound.

But some ringing is beautiful. One time I preached for a community Good Friday service. At the end of the service, the host minister dismissed everyone with some meaningful words of benediction, and then he went over to a large bell positioned in the front of the church building. With great reverence, he struck the bell three times. Simple as it was, the sound of that bell created a very worshipful moment. We had just heard about Jesus' sacrifice on the cross, and the whole congregation sat quietly for a minute or two, reflecting and praying as the sound of that bell rang in our ears and then faded into quietness.

On the campus of Cincinnati Bible College & Seminary, we used to have an old carillon, a set of bells that rang from the tower of the library building. Sometimes as you walked across campus, you would hear it playing a hymn. There was something peaceful and restful about it. The sound was soothing as it rang out across the valley from the top of the hill. I hadn't heard those bells in years. I asked the librarian, Jim Lloyd, "Do we still have the old bells? Can we still play them?"

He said the bells hadn't been used in a long time. Some of the students had complained that the bells woke them up too early in the morning! I asked him to ring the bells again once in awhile, and I told the students, "Whenever you hear the bells, remember that you need to take the gospel to someone who needs it."

An old song says, "There's a call comes ringing o'er the restless wave: Send the light, Send the light!" God calls us to go and make disciples, not to stay and make ourselves comfortable.

> **Before any church ever sponsored a "seeker service," the Lord came seeking us.**

The longest chapter in the Bible concludes with a prayer that says, "I have strayed like a lost sheep. Seek your servant" (Ps 119:176). God does seek us. Before anybody ever sought him, and before any church ever sponsored a "seeker service," the Lord came seeking us. In the Garden of Eden, after Adam and Eve sinned, God came seeking them and asking, "Where are you?" Jesus is such a good shepherd that he seeks us even when we've sinned again and again, and even if we're just one sheep that has strayed while 99 stayed with the shepherd. He came to seek and save the lost (Luke 19:10), and he sends us to seek them, too.

PRACTICAL WAYS TO "RING OUT THE GOOD NEWS"

- **Be a friend.** When it comes to evangelism, God's love is our secret weapon. Paul said, "You know how we lived among you for your sake" (1 Thess 1:5).

- **Open your home.** Hospitality opens doors to talk about the Lord in natural ways.

- **Visit others in their homes**—to get acquainted and to study the Word together. The apostle Paul taught "publicly and from house to house" (Acts 20:20).

- **Pray.** A friend of mine walks through his neighborhood and prays silently for his neighbors who live in each house. Over the years, he's led several of them to the Lord.

- **Give things away.** Christians should be known for our generosity and kindness. Offer a ride to school, a Bible, a book, a CD, a bit of time to listen. Be a generous tipper in restaurants and a generous server in community activities.

- **Write.** Use e-mail for dialogue about matters of faith. Or do it the old-fashioned way: Write a letter.
- **Be an example.** If you live consistently for Christ, eventually others will ask you "to give the reason for the hope that you have" (1 Pet 3:15). Be ready to tell them.
- **Reach out to an international student or a worker from another nation.** Every year more than 300,000 students come to the United States from other lands to study at American colleges and universities. Many are curious about spiritual things and hungry for friendship. Are there families in your neighborhood or some coworkers at your place of employment who came from a foreign land? Be a friend to them.
- **Invite.** Watch for natural opportunities to invite friends to attend church with you. Invite them to your home for dinner, to attend sports events with you, and to attend special programs at Thanksgiving, Christmas, or Easter.
- **Be available.** Get involved in activities that allow you to rub shoulders with the unchurched. Volunteer to help with school and community events. Play softball, basketball, or bowling—in the "regular" leagues, not only the church leagues.

Get on the Road to Gaza

One of my favorite Bible stories is the one in Acts chapter 8 about a believer named Philip. He was having great success leading people to Christ in Samaria. Strangely, right when large crowds were being baptized in Samaria, the Lord sent an angel to tell Philip it was time to leave. Instead of having Philip preach to the crowds in Samaria, God sent him down a desert road toward a town called Gaza.

Philip must have been wondering why the Lord would send him to such an obscure place. But while he walked along that road, he encountered a government leader from Africa who was riding in a chariot for the return trip to Ethiopia. The fellow in the chariot was in charge of the national treasury of Queen Candace, so you might expect he'd be going over a spreadsheet, making sure the numbers balanced in the Ethiopian budget. But instead, he was reading his Bible.

The story continues:

> The Spirit told Philip to catch up with the chariot. Philip ran up close and heard the man reading aloud from the book of Isaiah.
> Philip asked him, 'Do you understand what you are reading?'

An Unquenchable Love for Lost People 2

25

‡

C
H
A
P
T
E
R
2

The official answered, 'How can I understand unless someone helps me?' He then invited Philip to come up and sit beside him.

The man was reading the passage that said,

> 'He was led like a sheep on its way to be killed. He was silent as a lamb whose wool is being cut off, and he did not say a word. He was treated like a nobody and did not receive a fair trial. How can he have children, if his life is snatched away?'

The official said to Philip, 'Tell me, was the prophet talking about himself or about someone else?' So Philip began at this place in the Scriptures and explained the good news about Jesus.

As they were going along the road, they came to a place where there was some water. The official said, 'Look! Here is some water. Why can't I be baptized?' He ordered the chariot to stop. Then they both went down into the water, and Philip baptized him. After they had come out of the water, the Lord's Spirit took Philip away. The official never saw him again, but he was very happy as he went on his way (Acts 8:29-39, Contemporary English Version [CEV]).

Four key ingredients made the road to Gaza a place of joy that day. Whenever these four ingredients come together, great things happen.

A seeker + a servant + the Scriptures + the Savior . . . lead to someone saved.

The Ethiopian was the *seeker*—eager to worship God, aware of his spiritual hunger, but needing someone to teach him. Philip was the *servant*—available to go where God led him and equipped to share his faith when the opportunity arose. In this case, the *Scriptures* came from Isaiah chapter 53, powerful words of prophecy about the atoning death of Christ. The *Savior* is always Jesus, the perfect sacrifice for sin whose death and resurrection are the foundation of our forgiveness.

INGREDIENTS ON "THE ROAD TO GAZA"

A seeker, who is eager to learn about the Lord.

A servant, who is available to share what he knows.

The Scriptures, explained so the seeker can understand.

The Savior (Jesus), the focus of our message and the reason for a person's change of heart.

Pray that God will put you on the road to Gaza. Ask him to put you alongside people who are seeking to know him. Run alongside their chariots. Ask them good questions that get the conversation going. Sit with them. Listen to them. Point them to Jesus. Tell them how to respond to him in faith and in baptism.

An Unquenchable Love for Lost People

And don't leave out the need to repent from sin. In 1 Thessalonians 1:9, Paul says, "You turned to God from idols to serve the living and true God." Repentance is making a U-turn with your life. It's turning "from" something negative: "from idols." And it's turning "toward" something positive: "to serve the living and true God."

Idols take many different forms. False religion. Intellectual arrogance. Money and the things money can buy. Selfish pride. Gratification of the flesh. The desire to impress, to control, to own. It's a wonderful thing when people turn from the idols of their past and begin to serve "the living and true God."

In Lanett, Alabama, to speak at a church, I stayed at the home of a couple named Billy and Pat Parr. They're now retired, but very involved in their church. Pat didn't become a Christian until she was 36 years old. Her son was 14 then. The change in Pat's life was so dramatic, her son says, "Our house had always been dark. When Mom accepted Christ, it was as if the lights came on and our whole house became brighter." Now the Parrs use their house for youth gatherings and community outreach. On the Saturday after I stayed with them, Billy was having about 80 men from the community over to feed them sausage biscuits and to have a guest speaker tell them about Christ.

Who Needs the Gospel?

The Thessalonian Christians were having such a wide influence that Paul says, "your faith in God has become known everywhere" (1 Thess 1:8). Faith has a ripple effect on others who are touched by it.

> Faith has a ripple effect on others who are touched by it.

The ministry of evangelism starts in the nursery, as parents bring up their children in the nurture and admonition of the Lord. It extends to our neighborhoods, as we share the good news of Christ with friends, coworkers, and others in our local communities. And it reaches to the nations, as we send missionaries to preach the Word in the far reaches of the world.

The Thessalonian Christians had "turned to God from idols to serve the living and true God" (1 Thess 1:10). This is a decision countless others still need to make.

Our *families* need "the living and true God."

Do you have a parent, a grandparent, a brother or sister, or another relative who has never accepted Christ as Savior? It's sometimes difficult to share your faith with a family member, but where would the church be if Andrew hadn't brought his brother Simon Peter to meet Jesus (John 1:41,42)? Or if Timothy's mother Eunice and grandmother Lois had not taught him the Word of God from infancy (2 Tim 1:5; 3:15)? Parents should make the discipleship of our children a top priority (Deuteronomy 6:1-9; Eph 6:4). A wife married to an unsaved husband should witness to him by her respectful and loving behavior (1 Pet 3:1-6).

During a mission trip in Mexico City, Candy and I met a Christian woman named Juanita who had prayed for 14 years for her husband Jorge to accept Christ.

Over the years as she continued to pray for Jorge, her brother became a Christian, and she said, "That's good, Lord, but what about Jorge?" Her sister and daughter accepted the Lord, but she said, "That's good, Lord, but what about Jorge?"

Finally Jorge himself accepted Christ, and now he and Juanita are working together to plant a new church in their neighborhood.

Our families need the living and true God. If you are a parent, the work of evangelism starts with discipling your own children and leading them to Christ.

Our *neighbors* need "the living and true God."

A friend, Sam Kovacs, wrote and told me his story:

> A little over five years ago I wasn't active in any church and my wife and son were going to our local Catholic church every Sunday. I would lie in bed every time they went and would tell them to pray for me because "I probably needed it." I did feel bad because my six-year-old son didn't get to go with his daddy to church.
>
> At the time my wife, Meg, was reading a book called *Left Behind* and she kept bugging me to read it. The book made an impression on her heart to find a way to bring me closer to God, so she prayed for ways to approach me about it. Our initial conversations were focused on the positive result that would come out of my attending church; however she finally got frustrated and told me I was "going to Hell"!
>
> For the next few days I was very upset at what she said. At the time our good friends, Shannon and Tricia, extended an invitation to a new church called Horizon Christian Church. Meg called them and asked if she and Alex could attend Horizon that Sunday. . . . I decided it was time for me to go to church, so we joined them.
>
> The sermon that week was about seeing how God works through the Spirit. A few minutes into the sermon something came over me that I had never before experienced and I started tearing up. . . . It was one of the most moving sermons I'd ever heard. At the end of the sermon, family, friends and numerous other people saw that I was very shaken up.

As we exited the sanctuary one of the faithful rushed up to me and asked me a couple of questions and followed up with a real tough one: "Are you ready to accept Jesus as your Lord and Savior?" At that point I was both confused and mentally drained by the sermon. I very politely declined and told the man that I needed more time to think about what just happened to me.

Two days passed and all I could think about was Sunday's sermon and what had happened to me. I decided to call my next-door neighbor, Ned Campbell, who I knew was an elder of a Christian church. He immediately dropped what he was doing and came over. After a two-hour conversation about God, the Spirit, and Jesus Christ, Ned helped me see the light, and I most enthusiastically accepted Jesus as my Lord and Savior with his assistance. . . . My wife and I were baptized by Ned in a swimming pool at my parents' house in front of our friends and family. In addition, I have been in a men's Bible study group for the past five years and am a member of East 91st Street Christian Church.

The *hard-to-reach* need "the living and true God."

When Bob Yawberg preached at Broadway Christian Church in Fort Wayne, Indiana, his congregation spoke out against some adult bookstores in the neighborhood that sold hard core pornography. One Sunday a group of protesters showed up outside the church building carrying signs about free speech. One of the picketers was a man who dressed up like a nun and carried a sign that said, "It's 'nun' of your business what I read."

At church that morning Bob intentionally didn't even refer to the picketing. Instead, he just went ahead with the regular worship service as usual. He preached as planned on Jesus' words, "Lead us not into temptation, but deliver us from evil." It was a Sunday a lot of people remembered around that church.

Several years later, the young man who had carried the "It's 'nun' of your business" sign came to Bob and said, "Please forgive me." Bob said, "Of course." The man was then suffering in the last stages of disease brought on by the AIDS virus. Bob says, "At his request I lowered his thin body into the waters of baptism affirming in the name of Christ Jesus that his sins were forever forgiven. He later prepared a video testimony of faith in Christ to be shown at his memorial service."[1]

> In the first century nobody would have seemed harder to reach than Saul of Tarsus, but he became a Christian.

In the first century nobody would have seemed harder to reach than Saul of Tarsus, but he became a Christian. In the 1700s most people wouldn't have thought a slave trader named John Newton would ever turn to Christ, but he did, and he wrote the words to "Amazing Grace."

Lost people in unchurched areas of the United States and Canada need "the living and true God."

One of the most exciting things going on in America today is the dynamic movement to plant new churches in cities and towns where a large percentage of the population lacks any meaningful connection to the Lord and his church. New churches are springing up in urban centers like New York, Las Vegas, New Orleans, Seattle, and Pittsburgh.

In Romans 15:20, Paul wrote about his own heart for the lost. He said, "It has always been my ambition to preach the gospel where Christ was not known, so that I would not be building on someone else's foundation." Does that verse stir something in your heart? Like the apostle Paul, many Christians need to devote our lives to establishing new churches, taking the gospel where it's never been heard. Hundreds of new churches are needed in the urban centers of New England, the fast-growing cities of Arizona and Ontario, and in less populated areas like Saskatchewan and South Dakota.

> Like the apostle Paul, many Christians need to devote our lives to establishing new churches, taking the gospel where it's never been heard.

Lost people in other nations need "the living and true God."

When Jesus told his disciples in the first century to "go into all the world," they had never even seen a globe. They didn't realize how large the world is. They'd never heard of Australia, New Zealand, Japan, or Zimbabwe. And even if they could have heard about those places, how could they have traveled there?

Today it only takes about one day to fly anywhere in the world. By e-mail we can send messages instantly around the globe. Less than ten years after the invention of the commercial Internet, more e-mail and other data flow across the Internet than the amount of traffic generated by telephone calls.[2] Even with all the danger in today's world, there are unprecedented new opportunities to spread God's Word. This is an exciting time to be involved in global missions.

> Even with all the danger in today's world, there are unprecedented new opportunities to spread God's Word.

An Unquenchable Love for Lost People

Remember What Is at Stake

Paul wrote that we are waiting for God's "Son from heaven, whom he raised from the dead—Jesus, who rescues us from the coming wrath" (1 Thess 1:10).

I would rather not think about "the coming wrath." I'd rather not preach or write about it. I like to be positive and encouraging. I don't enjoy talking about Hell. It's not popular to preach about Judgment Day and the wrath of God, but the Bible says they are real.

We won't have an unquenchable love for lost people unless we realize that outside of Christ, we really are lost. A day of reckoning lies ahead with the God who created us. We have violated God's holy will, and unless our sins are forgiven, we must face God's holy wrath.

> **We won't have an unquenchable love for lost people unless we realize that outside of Christ, we really are lost.**

Jesus said, "A time is coming when all who are in their graves will hear his voice and come out—those who have done good will rise to live, and those who have done evil will rise to be condemned" (John 5:28,29). Hebrews 9:22 says, "It is appointed unto man to die once, and then comes the judgment." The book of Revelation tells about the great white throne of God, and a lake of fire where people are thrown if their names are not in God's book of life (Rev 20:11-15).

One of Satan's schemes is to make us doubt, or simply forget, the reality of divine judgment.

On September 14, 2001, three days after the 9/11 terrorist attacks, a group of musicians hosted a live TV show broadcast nationwide to raise money for the victims. Candles set a somber mood. Actors and musicians told moving stories about the brave people who gave their lives to rescue others. Most of the music consisted of soft, thoughtful songs accompanied by acoustic guitars and gentle keyboard numbers.

Neil Young sat down at the piano and sang John Lennon's "Imagine," one of the best-loved songs the Beatles ever produced. It has a haunting melody and lyrics about peace and the brotherhood of man. But the song's first line says, "Imagine there's no Heaven; it's easy if you try. No Hell below us; above us only sky."

As we watched TV, I turned to Candy and said incredulously, "This is supposed to *comfort* us?" We had just experienced one of the most traumatic days in American history. Thousands of people were dead. Millions were grieving. How would it help to think there is no Heaven or Hell? If there's no Heaven, there's no hope. If there's no Hell, there's

31

‡

C
H
A
P
T
E
R

An Unquenchable Love for Lost People   2

no ultimate justice for those who inflict such terrible harm on their fellow man.

> **Heaven and Hell are real. Life isn't a game.
> Eternity hangs in the balance.**

Heaven and Hell are real. Life isn't a game. Eternity hangs in the balance. If we get what our sins deserve, none of us will escape God's wrath. But look again at 1 Thessalonians 1:10. Jesus "rescues us from the coming wrath." God's wrath is what our sins deserve. God's grace removes his wrath from us—but only in Christ. Jesus rescues us from God's wrath because he endured God's wrath himself when he bore our sins on the cross (1 Pet 2:24,25; 3:18).

At First Christian Church in Chandler, Arizona, one Sunday a car broke down in the alley behind the church building. The driver jacked up the car and crawled underneath to fix it. Suddenly he began screaming for help. The jack had slipped and the car had pinned the man to the ground.

Someone called 911, and others gathered around the large car and strained their backs to lift it off the trapped man. Nurses from the congregation hurried to the scene to help. The man emerged from the experience scratched and shaken, but safe. When someone was in peril, everyone in the church did whatever they could to save him. That's what the church needs to do for those in spiritual peril as well.[3]

There are no cloned sheep in God's flock. Ask God to give you an unquenchable love for lost people. Find them. Love them. Pour your life into them. Pray for them. And let the good news ring!

> **There are no cloned sheep in God's flock.**

[1] Bob Yawberg, *Pastors in Prayer Ministry*, Vol. IV, no. 4.

[2] Sky Dayton, "Education in the Internet Age," *Imprimis* (May 2003) 2.

[3] Craig B. Larson, *750 Engaging Illustrations* (Grand Rapids: Baker, 2002) 174.

C
H
A
P
T
E
R

2 *An Unquenchable Love for Lost People*

Developing Unquenchable Faith

1. Are you currently building relationships with people who do not share your commitment to Christ?

2. Tell about a time when you were:
   a. The "seeker" someone led to Christ, or . . .
   b. The "servant" God used to lead a "seeker" to Christ.

3. How often do you think about Heaven and Hell? Do you think most people give serious consideration to the reality of divine judgment? Do you?

4. List three of your relatives, friends, neighbors, or coworkers who need the Lord. Talk with your group about what you could do to engage them in conversation about Christ.

5. Close your group by praying for specific opportunities to share God's love with non-Christians in the coming week.

Memory Verse
1 Thess 1:8

The Lord's message rang out from you . . . your faith in God has become known everywhere.

CHAPTER THREE

AN UNQUENCHABLE DESIRE TO BE A GODLY LEADER

1 THESSALONIANS 2:1-12

When I ministered with East 91st Street Christian Church in Indianapolis, one evening Candy and I were visiting with people in the hallway after a Christmas program.

We started talking with a little four-year-old girl named Samantha and her parents, who call her "Sam." She looked up at me and said, "I know you. You're the man who teaches us on Sundays."

I was glad she recognized me. I nodded, "Yes, that's right, Sam."

She looked back at me and said, "You tell LONG stories!"

I replied, "Is that your own opinion, or is that what you hear your *parents* saying?"

We had a good laugh together, and I promised Sam I'd make sure my stories didn't go too long in the future. But our little encounter reminded me what a difficult responsibility it is to be a leader.

Bob Russell, senior minister at Southeast Christian Church in Louisville, Kentucky, received a note from a third-grader named Kenny. The note said, "To Bob Russell. You have to be brave to be able to stand in front of thousands of people. I am glad you're a preacher at this church, and I think you do a wonderful job. I am praying that one of these times you won't mess up."

> In the right situation, most Christians can exercise leadership—and the Lord expects us to do so.

It's tough to be a leader. And yet, God still calls us to lead. Do you have an unquenchable desire to be a leader? Perhaps you do not think of yourself as a leader at all, but in the right situation, most Christians can exercise leadership—and the Lord expects us to do so.

A Closer Look at Leadership

Leadership is influence. If you influence even one other person, you're a leader. If you teach a child in a Sunday school class, you're a leader. If you're a parent, your children look to you for leadership. If you're a Christian, by your example you will draw your friends closer to Christ or drive them farther away from him.

> **If you influence even one other person, you're a leader.**

Leadership is a gift. You may be a "born leader," someone who has always aspired to lead others. I heard about a young man who was talking to an army recruiter. The recruiter said that, since doing away with the draft, the government has gone to an all-volunteer army. The young man said, "Great! I volunteer to be a general!"

Some of us naturally gravitate toward leadership. Perhaps for as long as you can remember, you've been the captain of your basketball team, the first chair in the orchestra, or the president of your class at school. On the other hand, some are reluctant leaders. Moses and Jeremiah initially lacked self-confidence. They balked at God's call and tried to avoid leadership because they didn't really want to do what God was asking them to do. Evidently Timothy struggled with the burden of leadership, for Paul urged him to "fan into flame the gift of God" and reminded him that "God did not give us a spirit of timidity, but a spirit of power, of love and of self-discipline" (2 Tim 1:7).

> **Leadership is a gift, but it's also a learned skill.**

Leadership is a gift, but it's also a learned skill—and sometimes it's simply the right person willing to do the right things in the right place at the right time. A leader makes things happen; he isn't satisfied with the status quo. A real leader brings improvement and makes things better. John Maxwell says, "The pessimist complains about the wind. The optimist expects the wind to change. The leader adjusts the sails." A leader has a compass in his head and a magnet in his heart—he knows where he's going and he's able to draw others to pursue the vision too.

Great Leaders

When you consider great leadership, maybe you think of a coach like Tom Landry or John Wooden. Or an entrepreneur who builds a successful business or turns a struggling company around, like Bill Gates, Henry Ford, or Lee Iacocca. Maybe you think of a person who inspires social change, like Mother Teresa or Martin Luther King.

Or maybe you think of someone whose leadership has touched your life directly. An inspiring boss. A teacher who shaped your thinking and your character. A minister, elder, or youth leader at church who encouraged you to grow in your faith. A parent or grandparent who led by example.

You probably can think of some bad leaders, too. A corrupt politician who lies to get votes. A coach who uses profanity and bullies his players. A boss who mistreats his employees. An ineffective teacher who doesn't seem to care about the subject or the students. A religious leader who fleeces the flock instead of caring for it.

The Bible tells about different kinds of leaders—both good ones and bad ones. Deborah was a wise woman who led during the time of the Judges. Joshua and Gideon were men of faith who organized and led the armies of God. The Bible tells about selfish, wicked rulers like Ahab and Jezebel, and about faithful Daniel, who rose to a high position in government without compromising his faith and values.

One of my favorite biblical examples of leadership is David, who led armies to battle and organized choirs to sing and worship God. One time when David was on the run from King Saul, he hid in a cave. Four hundred men came to join David, and the Bible says, "All those who were in distress or in debt or discontented gathered around him" (1 Samuel 22:2). How would you like that for your support group? "In distress, in debt, and discontented"? Those 400 men were dysfunctional with a capital D!

But the Bible goes on to say, "And [David] became their leader" (1 Sam 22:2). By the end of David's life, he had a group of loyal, heroic soldiers around him who were nicknamed "David's mighty men" (2 Sam 23:8-39). I wonder: Did some of these "mighty men" come from the distressed, discontented group mentioned earlier? Take some people with potential, expose them to good leadership, and eventually God will shape them into "mighty men and women" who can do great things.

The Greatest Leader

The greatest leader who ever walked the earth is Jesus Christ. He is the Master of the Ministers, the Pastor of the Pastors, the Head of the Body, the "great Shepherd of the sheep" (Heb 13:20).

Jesus modeled visionary leadership. His purpose was clear: to seek and save the lost. His mission was comprehensive: to make disciples all over the world. His vision was bold: to establish a church that would bash down the gates of Hell. His values were unmistakable: to speak the truth and act in love in every situation. His motivation was pure: to accomplish the will of the Father. His passion was selfless and unquenchable, for he came not "to be served, but to serve, and to give his life as a ransom for many" (Mark 10:45).

Jesus modeled visionary leadership.

Jesus redefined leadership, telling his disciples, "You know that the rulers of the Gentiles lord it over them, and their high officials exercise authority over them. Not so with you" (Matt 20:25,26). Jesus rejected the secular model that says you get to be a leader by being self-promoting, power-hungry, and autocratic. He said, "Whoever wants to become great among you must be your servant, and whoever wants to be first must be slave of all" (Mark 10:43,44).

He rejected the secular model that you get to be a leader by being self-promoting, power-hungry, and autocratic.

He said, "All authority in Heaven and on earth has been given to me," but he humbly washed his disciples' dirty feet. He taught with incredible insight, yet he allowed people to question him. He accepted people just as they were, but he also inspired them to become better than they were. He led by example. He practiced what he preached.

Jesus recruited, trained, equipped, and unleashed a little band of committed men and women who literally changed the world. Two thousand years later, the world still feels the influence of Jesus' leadership.

HOW CAN JESUS' LEADERSHIP INFLUENCE YOU?

- If you're self-centered, he will lead you to care about others.
- If you're lonely, he will give you a place of significance in his family.
- If you're afraid, he will give you courage.
- If you're worried, he will give you peace.
- If you're bored, he will inspire you to tackle a new adventure.
- If you're suffering, he will give you hope and strength.
- If you're weary of the rat race, Jesus can fill your heart with a new sense of purpose.

Six Characteristics of a Godly Leader

The Lord shaped and molded the apostle Paul into a great leader. In 1 Thessalonians chapter two, Paul opens his heart and describes six marks of a godly leader that can help us grow in our own leadership roles.

1. A godly leader perseveres in spite of criticism and hardship.

Paul reminds the Thessalonians, "You know, brothers, that our visit to you was not a failure. We had previously suffered and been insulted in Philippi . . . but with the help of our God we dared to tell you his gospel in spite of strong opposition" (vv. 1,2).

Acts chapter 16 tells about the suffering Paul experienced in Philippi. He and Silas cast a demon out of a slave-girl there. This made her masters angry because the girl's fortune-telling had been their source of income, and she had earned them a lot of money. So they falsely accused Paul and Silas, had them stripped and beaten with rods (wooden clubs, like baseball bats), and then had them thrown into prison and their feet fastened in stocks.

About midnight Paul and Silas were praying and singing hymns to God. Suddenly an earthquake shook the prison doors open and loosed the chains of the prisoners. In the middle of the night, the apostles spoke the Word of the Lord to the jailer and his family and baptized them into Christ before the night was over. Paul and Silas suffered physical abuse in Philippi. They were insulted. They faced strong opposition. But through it all, they dared to say and do what was right.

When I was a boy, my family's farm had its own well and its own water supply. The county decided to modernize and install a pipeline. For a moderate fee, any farmer who chose to do so could hook his plumbing system to the pipeline and receive water from a public utility company.

Many local farmers opposed the idea. They didn't want anyone digging up the roads and installing a pipeline so they could drink "chlorinated city water." But my grandfather was for it. He thought the waterline would be good for property values, and it would save us from worrying about our wells going dry during the hot summer months. So Grandpa went around to the farmers and tried to enlist their support.

When that pipeline was installed, Grandpa took a lot of criticism, and I didn't like hearing negative things said about him. Grandpa, though, just shrugged it off. He told me, "David, the only people who don't get criticized are the ones who never accomplish anything." Years later, every farmer in that area is glad the pipeline was installed, but somebody had to take the lead and get the job done in spite of the criticism.

An Unquenchable Desire to Be a Godly Leader

Wayne Smith used to say, "On a football team, if you carry the ball you're going to be tackled." Public scrutiny is one of the prices of leadership. Former major league umpire Doug Harvey said, "When I am right, no one remembers. When I am wrong, no one forgets."

You think you face a lot of criticism? When Gerald Ford was president of the United States he pardoned former president Richard Nixon for his role in the Watergate scandal. Ford received 273,331 cards, letters, and telegrams in response—most of which were negative, and many of them from high-ranking government officials. (Many of the critical letters remain on public display at the Gerald R. Ford Museum in Grand Rapids, Michigan.)

A leader must persevere in spite of criticism and hardship.

It's Not the Critic Who Counts

Theodore Roosevelt, the 26th president of the United States, said: "It is not the critic who counts, not the man who points out how the strong man stumbles or where the doer of deeds could have done them better. The credit belongs to the man who is actually in the arena, whose face is marred by dust and sweat and blood, who strives valiantly, who errs and comes up short again and again because there is no effort without error and shortcomings, who knows the great devotion, who spends himself in a worthy cause, who at the best knows in the end the high achievement of triumph and who at worst, if he fails while daring greatly, knows his place shall never be with those timid and cold souls who know neither victory nor defeat."

– Speech at the Sorbonne, Paris, France (April 23, 1910).

---

2. A godly leader is authentic.

"The appeal we make does not spring from error or impure motives, nor are we trying to trick you" (v. 3). "You know we never used flattery, nor did we put on a mask to cover up greed" (v. 5). J.B. Phillips translates this passage, "Our conduct is absolutely above board."

The apostle Paul was transparent, honest, and authentic. He was exactly what he appeared to be.

The world has seen enough religious hypocrisy.

The world has seen enough religious hypocrisy. The Lord doesn't want us to manipulate people or put on masks to cover up who we really are. "A malicious man disguises himself with his lips, but in his heart he harbors deceit. Though his speech is charming, do not believe him" (Prov 26:24,25).

In ancient Rome, when sculptors carved statues out of marble, sometimes the stone would crack. Unscrupulous sculptors would fill the cracks with wax so no one could see the imperfections. The problem was, in time the wax would dry and flake away, and the buyer was left with a flawed statue. To certify the quality and integrity of their work, reputable sculptors came up with a designation called *"sine cera,"* which literally means "without wax." That's where we get our word "sincere." Christians need to be "without wax," not just playing a role to cover up our imperfections. Others can tell whether or not our faith is authentic.

When I was a teenager, a traveling evangelist visited our church for a weeklong revival. He was a very effective preacher, and I admired his skill in teaching the Bible.

One evening before church, I saw him in the parking lot, and I told him I was puzzled by something he had said in his message the previous evening. It was just a Bible question I had been wondering about. I was stunned when he answered me harshly. He told me that what he said came straight from the Bible, and if I didn't like it, I'd better adjust my thinking because he wasn't going to change his mind. His words wounded me deeply, right at a time when I was struggling with doubt and trying to find my way as a young Christian. The problem was not just what he said, but that his attitude was so harsh and unkind. The way he treated me didn't match with the loving, wise image he portrayed from the pulpit.

If you want to be a godly leader, be authentic.

William Barclay once said, "A man's message is always heard in the context of his character." If you want to be a godly leader, be authentic. Don't just play a role and pretend to be something you're not.

GOOD SHEPHERDS
The Bible contains several word-pictures for the mature believers who lead God's people. The word "elder" underscores their experience and wisdom, and "shepherd" or "pastor" emphasizes their love for the sheep under their care. The Bible makes it plain that a leader's character (who he is as a person) cannot be separated from his work (what he does to lead). See Psalm 23:1-6; Ezekiel 34:1-31; Acts 20:28; and 1 Peter 5:1-4.

An Unquenchable Desire to Be a Godly Leader

3. A godly leader seeks to please God, not men.

"We are not trying to please men but God, who tests our hearts" (v. 4). "We were not looking for praise from men, not from you or anyone else" (v. 6).

People can be very hard to please. In one church where I served as minister, we installed a new baptistery, and then it was time to install a curtain in front of it. Some members of the congregation wanted a brown curtain, others wanted a green curtain, some wanted a gold curtain, and some didn't want a curtain at all.

In another church, we took a poll about worship styles. Some members wanted traditional music because "contemporary music isn't very spiritual." Others wanted contemporary music because "the Holy Spirit can't work through that traditional stuff."

I quickly discovered it was impossible to please everyone. Even Jesus didn't please everyone. Shouldn't we be more concerned about leading others to Christ and baptizing them than we are about what color the baptistery curtain should be? And shouldn't we be so hungry to come before the throne of God in worship that we will humbly do whatever we can to sing his praise?

It's hard to please others. And it's *wrong* to please them if, in the process, we displease God. It's nice to be liked. But we shouldn't compromise our principles in order to be popular. Some will not be pleased if we teach the biblical truth that Jesus Christ is the only way to be saved (John 14:6). But we must be true to the Lord, not men. If we dare to challenge the materialistic values, the loose sexual standards, or the pridefulness of our culture, some won't be pleased with us.

> **Don't make it your goal to please the sheep.**
> **Make it your goal to please the Shepherd.**

The apostle Paul wrote that "the time will come when men will not put up with sound doctrine. Instead, to suit their own desires, they will gather around them a great number of teachers to say what their own itching ears want to hear. They will turn their ears away from the truth and turn aside to myths." How should a godly leader respond? "But you, keep your head in all situations, endure hardship, do the work of an evangelist, discharge all the duties of your ministry" (2 Tim 4:4,5).

Don't make it your goal to please the sheep. Make it your goal to please the Shepherd.

4. A godly leader leads by example, not merely by words.

"We loved you so much that we were delighted to share with you not only the gospel of God but our lives as well, because you had become so dear to us" (v. 8). Paul didn't just preach to them; he lived with them. If you want to be a godly leader, don't just share the gospel; share your life.

> **If you want to be a godly leader,**
> **don't just share the gospel; share your life.**

Don't just tell people they need to love each other. Demonstrate it by loving your own family and by being a true friend. Don't just talk about how Christians need to pray. Develop your own private prayer life and spend time in prayer with others. Don't just speak out against sin. With the Holy Spirit's help, make it your goal to live a holy life and grow more like Christ.

Jackie Long served as my administrative assistant for awhile at East 91st Street Christian Church. She had served in the church for many years. When she retired, a large crowd gathered to pay tribute to her and thank her for her years of service. Jackie is the kind of person who is always there when someone needs a word of advice, a prayer, some benevolent help, or someone to talk to. Over the years, she not only has shared the gospel with others; she has shared her life.

When I heard that Jackie's mother had died, I immediately drove to the hospital. Jackie and I stood alone in the room next to the bed where her mother's body lay. We prayed together by the bedside, and after a while there was nothing else to do and it was time to go. Jackie gathered up her mother's things and put them into a plastic bag. As we walked out to the parking lot, she said, "At a time like this it's good to know there's more to a person's life than just what you can stuff into a plastic bag!"

Many people might not think of Jackie as a leader, but I do. When her faith was on the line, she led not just by her words, but by her example.

5. A godly leader demonstrates a strong personal work ethic.

"We worked night and day in order not to be a burden to anyone while we preached the gospel of God to you" (v. 9).

Paul was a tent-maker by trade. In those days tents were made of leather or from a canvaslike material made from goats' hair. Tent-making was hard work. But when circumstances required it, Paul made tents to support himself so he could preach the gospel without depending on the church to pay his salary.

According to the Bible, it's permissible for a church leader to be paid, but it's not always possible. In some cases, missionaries and church planters need to be tent-makers and make their living some other way instead of being paid by the church. In any event, if you want to be a leader, you must be willing to work hard. It's part of the price you pay to lead.

> If you want to be a leader, you must work hard. Serving the Lord is too important to be halfhearted about it.

Some church leaders work too hard.[1] But you won't lead if you're lazy, and serving the Lord is too important to be halfhearted about it. Ministry can't be confined to a 40-hour work week. There are times when a preacher needs to be at the hospital by 6:00 a.m. to pray with a patient before surgery. There are times when an elders meeting or a youth group function will keep a church leader up late at night. In a rural community where farmers are up at the crack of dawn to milk their cows, a preacher who doesn't get to the office till 9:00 in the morning will find it hard to gain the community's respect.

Proverbs 14:23 says, "All hard work brings a profit, but mere talk leads only to poverty."

6. A godly leader treats people like family.

"We were gentle among you, like a mother caring for her little children" (v. 7). "We dealt with each of you as a father deals with his own children, encouraging, comforting and urging you to live lives worthy of God" (vv. 11,12).

I've always pictured the apostle Paul as a rugged sort of guy with a keen mind, a witty tongue, a bit of a temper, and some scars on his body from the shipwrecks and beatings he had endured. This passage doesn't seem to fit his macho image. Here's masculine, hard-nosed Paul comparing himself to a nursing mother and a wise, strong, encouraging father.

> Godly leadership doesn't mean bossing people around.

Godly leadership doesn't mean bossing people around. In the church, the model for leadership isn't the military or the corporate world—it's a healthy family. That's why Scripture emphasizes leadership in the home as a prerequisite for leadership in the church. "If anyone does not know how to manage his own family, how can he take care of God's church?" (1 Tim 3:5). The home is where God wants us

An Unquenchable Desire to Be a Godly Leader

to learn basic values, and it's where we can learn about leadership from moms and dads who love us, guide us, and correct us.

What Kind of Leader Will You Be?

Our nation needs men and women of integrity who will serve God and lead our communities with honor and dignity. Our families need moms and dads who will love each other and bring up their children with gentle love and firm discipline. Our churches need people with servants' hearts who will step up and lead Bible classes, youth groups, and children's ministries—and others who are willing to serve as preachers, elders, deacons, and ministry leaders.

But before you become a leader, you have to be a follower. Are you really following Jesus? Have you submitted your life to him and made him Lord of all?

When the Indianapolis 500 takes place on Memorial Day weekend, 33 cars speed around the track—not at a comfortable 55 miles per hour, but at four times that pace: 220 miles per hour. During time trials prior to the race, each driver tries to get the "pole position." They want the inside track so they can start in first place. That's where a lot of us would like to be—in the lead, in first place, on the inside track.

But for Jesus, "pole position" meant being nailed to the cross. As the greatest leader, the Good Shepherd laid down his life in an incredible act of sacrifice for the sheep. If we want to be good and effective leaders ourselves, we must learn to be more like Jesus.

---

[1] For a discussion of the problem of imbalance in the leader's personal life, see my earlier book, *Growing Churches, Growing Leaders: How to Lead a Growing Church and Live a Balanced Life* (Joplin, MO: College Press, 1994).

Developing Unquenchable Faith

1. Do you think of yourself as a leader? Why, or why not? Do *others* think of you as a leader?

2. Who is the best leader you have ever met? What made him or her so effective as a leader?

3. Have you ever faced "strong opposition" like the kind the apostle Paul mentions in 1 Thessalonians 2:2? How do you handle criticism and personal attacks?

4. Have you ever been hurt by a leader who lacked integrity? If so, what did you learn from that experience?

5. The apostle Paul compares his leadership style to "a mother caring for her little children" (1 Thess 2:7) and the way "a father deals with his own children" (v. 11). What parallels do you see between a healthy family and a healthy church? In practical terms, what might this mean about the way church leaders do their jobs?

6. Conclude your small group time by praying by name for some leaders you know (in government, in your church, in your community, and in your families).

Memory Verse 1 Thess 1:11-12

For you know that we dealt with each of you as a father deals with his own children, encouraging, comforting and urging you to live lives worthy of God, who calls you into his kingdom and glory.

CHAPTER FOUR

AN UNQUENCHABLE DEVOTION TO GOD'S WORD

1 THESSALONIANS 2:13

I met Feng Min at a dinner for international students at the University of Cincinnati. Just a few days before, he and his wife had come to the United States from China. Since the meal was sponsored by Christians, we bowed our heads and prayed before the food was served. Feng Min asked me what we were doing. It turns out, he had never seen anyone pray like that before.

For dessert we were served fortune cookies that contained Scripture verses printed on slips of paper. When Feng Min asked me what they were, I explained they were sayings found in the Bible. He looked back at me with a blank stare. I said, "Have you ever seen a Bible before?" He said, "No." I had the privilege of giving Feng Min his very first copy of God's Word. By the look on his face, you'd have thought I had given him a brick of gold.

The Bible is more valuable than gold. The psalmist praised God for his Word and said, "I love your commands more than gold, more than pure gold" (Ps 119:127).

The Value of the Bible

The Bible Is a Gift for All Ages.

When my granddaughter was less than a year old, she already had her own *Baby's First Bible*. My great-grandfather read the Bible through every year. When he died, they found him sitting in his chair with the Bible in his hand, clutching a page from Second Kings.

Maybe you've heard about the boy who asked his brother, "Why does Grandma read the Bible so much?"

His brother answered, "Maybe she's studying for her finals!"

The Bible Is a Gift for All Circumstances.

I have a friend who rides the Long Island Railroad into New York City every day. He uses his commuting time to read the Bible.

A preacher friend of mine ministers to his wife, who has Alzheimers disease. When she reached the point where she could no longer speak, she still would respond with smiles and tears when her husband read the Bible to her—especially the Psalms.

The Bible Is a Gift for All Cultures.

When I preached at a church in Seoul, Korea, they asked me to take my shoes off first out of reverence for God. It was the only time I've ever preached in my sock feet.

In Ethiopia I had dinner at the home of a man named Sima who told me he had to hide his Bible for 17 years so the Communists wouldn't confiscate it or imprison him for owning it. The Bible comforted him and gave him spiritual liberty even when outwardly he was not a free man.

The Bible Is a Gift That Comes in Many Packages.

In ancient times Scripture was written on leather scrolls or leaves of papyrus. Today there are big, heavy Bibles that look impressive on pulpits, museum shelves, and coffee tables, and others so small you can stick them into your pocket or purse, or read them from a CD you slip into your computer. Years ago a friend gave me a microform slide produced by the NCR Company called "The Smallest Bible in the World." It reproduces 1,245 pages of the Bible—773,746 words—on one tiny plastic slide, one inch square. The accompanying instruction booklet says if you put it under a microscope you can read "both the Old and New Testaments in easy-to-read type."

The Bible can even be found in outer space. In 1970, a microfilm packet containing Genesis 1:1 in 16 languages and a complete *Revised Standard Version* Bible were placed on the moon by astronaut Edgar Mitchell of the Apollo 14 moon mission.

The Bible Is a Gift for All Languages and Dialects.

In the 1700s the French skeptic Voltaire predicted that within 100 years the Bible would be extinct. He said, "Twelve men wrote it up; I shall write it down. It shall soon be a forgotten book." But within a few years of Voltaire's death, the Geneva Bible Society began using Voltaire's house and his printing press to publish Bibles, and eventually his house became the headquarters for the British and Foreign Bible Society.

In 1999, a book was published called *1,000 Years, 1,000 People: Ranking the Men and Women Who Shaped the Millennium*. A lot of famous names made the list, including: Albert Einstein, George Washington, Queen Elizabeth, Christopher Columbus, Isaac Newton, and Ludwig van Beethoven. But the person identified as the most influential individual of the millennium was Johannes Gutenberg, the German inventor who used the movable-type printing press to publish the first major book ever printed: a Bible published in 1456. Gutenberg's work forever changed the way information would be communicated and was a major factor in the Protestant Reformation, which began to put God's Word into the hands of the people.

The modern print media started with Scripture. You can still see an

> **The modern print media started with Scripture.**

original copy of Gutenberg's Bible in the Library of Congress in Washington, D.C. Gutenberg said, "Yes, it is a press, certainly, but a press from which shall soon flow, in inexhaustible streams, the most abundant and most marvelous liquor that has ever flowed to relieve the thirst of men! Through it, God will spread his word. A spring of pure truth shall flow from it; like a new star it shall scatter the darkness of ignorance, and cause a light heretofore unknown to shine amongst men."[1]

Since Gutenberg's Bible rolled off the press, over 12 billion Bibles and New Testaments have been printed and distributed.

GOD'S WORD FOR ALL LANGUAGES

Languages currently spoken in the world: 6,809.

Languages that have Scripture: 2,287. Of these, 392 have an adequate Bible, 1,012 have an adequate New Testament, and 883 have at least one book of the Bible.

Number of people who don't have any Scripture ("Bible-less people groups"): 380 million. 250 million don't have the Scriptures or a translation program; 130 million don't have the Scriptures but do have a program in progress.

Total number of languages in which Bible translation is currently in progress: About 1,500.

*Source: Wycliffe International, Orlando, Florida (**www.wycliffe.org**).*

An Unquenchable Devotion to God's Word

The Bible Is a Gift with Unmistakable Power.

Some Bibles are well worn from constant use. Others have pages that stick together because they've hardly been opened. But regardless of the size of the volume, there's no mistaking the spiritual power of the Book. Jesus prayed and said, "Your word is truth" (John 17:17). David wrote, "The words of the Lord are flawless, like silver refined in a furnace of clay, purified seven times" (Ps 12:6).

The apostle Paul wrote, "And we also thank the Lord continually because, when you received the word of God, which you heard from us, you accepted it not as the word of men, but as it actually is, the word of God, which is at work in you who believe" (1 Thess 2:13).

Writing around A.D. 95, Clement of Rome said, "You have studied the Holy Scriptures, which are true and inspired by the Holy Spirit. You know nothing contrary to justice or truth has been written in them."[2]

Sir Walter Scott wrote, "The most learned, acute, and diligent student cannot, in the longest life, obtain an entire knowledge of the Bible. The more deeply he works the mine, the richer he finds the ore."[3]

Why should we have an unquenchable devotion to the Word of God? Is it reasonable to agree with the apostle Paul's declaration that the gospel he proclaimed is not merely the "word of men" but "the word of God"?

It Tells about the Facts We Need to Know

Deuteronomy 29:29 says, "The secret things belong to the Lord our God, but the things revealed belong to us and to our children forever, that we may follow all the words of this law." There are many things we will never understand, but God has revealed what we need to know.

Facts about Science

How many stars are in the heavens? The ancient astronomer Ptolemy said there were 1,056. Look up at an unpolluted, cloudless sky at 2:00 in the morning, and that's about how many you can see with the naked eye. But now we know there are far more stars than any of us can count. Yet, the very first book of the Bible tells how God took a childless man named Abram outside and said, "Look up at the heavens and count the stars—if indeed you can count them." Then God said, "So shall your offspring be" (Genesis 15:5). Later God compared the huge number of Abraham's offspring to the grains of sand on the seashore, which are more like the number of stars in the heavens.

Long before anyone understood the scientific reason for it, God told his people that the "life of the flesh is in the blood" (Leviticus. 17:11,

14). He told them to let their land rest and rotate their crops (Leviticus 25). In Isaiah 40:22 he hinted about the shape of the earth when he referred to the "circle of the earth." Job 26:7 sounds like it's talking about outer space when it says God "suspends the earth over nothing."

How do you explain the order and complexity of the universe? The Bible explains it in the first verse: "In the beginning God created the heavens and the earth" (Gen 1:1).

How do you explain the intricate design of the human body? The Bible says we are "fearfully and wonderfully made" (Ps 139:14). The DNA in a tiny fertilized human egg contains more carefully-coded information than a stack of encyclopedias. Yet the DNA filaments necessary to specify every unique human being alive today would only weigh about $1/15$ the weight of a postage stamp.[4] We have 27 small bones in each hand and wrist, with 30 muscles that move the bones of each hand. Chimpanzees or gorillas cannot do the wide variety of things we can do with our hands (thread needles, play the piano, tie and untie knots, finger-pick a guitar, or paint a portrait) even if they wanted to.[5]

The Bible's main purpose isn't to be a science textbook. As someone said, "The Bible tells how to go to Heaven, not how the heavens go." But in the process, it tells us useful facts about science.

Facts about History

The Bible isn't filled with fairy tales. Its authors recorded historical truth handed down by "eyewitnesses and servants of the word" who "carefully investigated" what they observed and wrote "an orderly account" for succeeding generations to read (Luke 1:1-3).[6]

> **The Bible isn't filled with fairy tales.**

Centuries before Christ, the prophet Amos spoke out against the lazy Israelites who lounged around on their beds of ivory (Amos 6:4). Archaeologists have found beautiful pieces of ivory from that very time period—some carved into intricate furniture decorations shaped like lions and bulls, and an ivory bed covered with carvings of lotus flowers and ivory plaques.[7]

The Associated Press reported that an ancient sandstone tablet was found in Jerusalem that refers to King Joash. In the inscription, Joash tells priests to take "holy money . . . to buy quarry stones and timber and copper and labor to carry out the duty with faith." It says if the work is completed well, "the Lord will protect his people with blessing." This fits nicely with the biblical account found in 2 Kings 12.[8]

An article in *U. S. News & World Report* tells how a team of archaeologists working at the site of the ancient Israelite city of Dan found a piece of a monument from the ninth century B.C. that commemorates a military victory of the king of Damascus. It mentions "the king of Israel" and "the house of David," strong nonbiblical evidence for the historical accuracy of the Bible.[9]

In the 1990s, construction workers widening a road near Jerusalem uncovered an ossuary (a limestone burial box) that contains an inscription identifying the body placed in it as that of "Joseph, Son of Caiaphas," the high priest who presided at the trial of Jesus.[10] Another ossuary was found recently with an inscription that mentions "James, son of Joseph, brother of Jesus."[11]

In the year 2000, Candy and I celebrated our 25th wedding anniversary by traveling to the Holy Land. The historical reality of the Bible came alive to us as we stood in the places where so many of the biblical stories took place. In the Cairo Museum in Egypt, we saw the gold found in King Tut's tomb. We visited the pyramids and saw firsthand why it took such courage for Moses to stand against Pharaoh and demand that he set God's people free. We climbed Mount Sinai, and on top of the mountain as the sun went down, we read the Ten Commandments and prayed and sang praises to God.

In Israel, we sailed on a boat on the Sea of Galilee, where Jesus stilled the storm and walked on water. We visited the synagogue in Capernaum, a site where Jesus taught and healed the sick. We visited the Jordan River, where Jesus was baptized. At Caesarea, we saw enormous stone aqueducts built by King Herod. In Jerusalem, we participated in a Sunday morning communion service in the Garden of Gethsemane where Jesus prayed on the night before he died on the cross.

In Corinth, we saw a pavement that mentions Erastus, a Christian and a public official mentioned by name in Romans 16:23. In Athens, I stood on the Areopagus (Mars Hill) and read the sermon Paul preached there (recorded in Acts 17).

In the 1950s, historians published interviews about the Civil War with some of the few people still around who had been alive back in the 1860s. They wanted to make sure their eyewitness testimony was recorded before it was too late. In the Holocaust Museum in Jerusalem you can see heartbreaking photographs, letters, and other pieces of evidence that document the atrocities the Nazis brought about on the Jews of Europe. Jewish leaders are concerned because the generation of people who suffered under the Nazis is gradually dying off. Before these eyewitnesses are gone, they want to make sure history has a thorough record of what they saw and what they suffered.

An Unquenchable Devotion to God's Word **4**

The New Testament was written within the lifetime
of the eyewitnesses who saw Jesus firsthand.

The New Testament was written within the lifetime of the eyewitnesses who saw Jesus firsthand. Late in the first century, the apostle John said he was recording what "we have heard, which we have seen with our eyes, which we have looked at and our hands have touched—this we proclaim concerning the Word of life" (1 John 1:1).

The Bible tells us historical facts we need to know.

Facts about God

Something in the human spirit tells us there is a God, but we need the Bible to tell us what kind of God he is.

Nature tells us that God exists, but we need the Bible to show us he is not only a God of power and order, but also a God of love and redemption.

Instinct tells us to pray, but we need the Bible to tell us that God hears and answers our requests.

Our hearts long for eternal life, but we need the Bible to tell us how to be saved.

Something in the human spirit tells us there is a God,
but we need the Bible to tell us what kind of God he is.

To satisfy the human mind and heart, a worldview has to offer a reasonable answer for several important questions: (1) the question of origins: *Where did we come from?* (2) the question of sin and suffering: *What has gone wrong?* (3) the question of purpose: *Why are we here?* (4) the question of destiny: *Is there any hope?* The Bible deals with each of these fundamental questions with unsurpassed wisdom. It tells us the facts we need to know.

It Tells about the Lives We Need to Live

52

‡

C
H
A
P
T
E
R

An ancient monk once observed, "The nature of water is soft, that of stone is hard; but if a bottle is hung above the stone, allowing the water to fall drop by drop, it wears away the stone. So it is with the Word of God; it is soft and our heart is hard, but the man who hears the Word of God often, opens his heart to the fear of God."

God's Word is "solid food" that gives us "teaching about righteousness" and trains us "to distinguish good from evil" (Heb 5:14).

My friend Bob Walters wrote me a letter and said:

4   *An Unquenchable Devotion to God's Word*

It was one year ago on Sunday, November 18, 2001, that you baptized me. That date is now a special anniversary. As I praise the Lord every day, I thank him for the message he sent to me though you.

I've read the Bible from Genesis to Revelation, made it to all but a half-dozen sessions of the Wednesday night "Through the Bible in 2002" series at our church . . . read Scripture every day, pray deeply and frequently for all things great and small, and have been blessed with opportunities to share my faith publicly. I've met the most interesting people. We go to church as a family every Sunday. I'm bursting with gratitude to the Lord, and can't wait to learn more.

Yet the most important thing I've learned is that his love endures forever. I feel his blessings every day. I see them in the Word, I see them in my children's eyes, I feel them in the Holy Spirit. I have found great comfort in the Word this year, and I will be grateful as that gift resides in me the rest of my life and beyond.

Ecclesiastes 12:11 says, "The words of the wise are like goads, their collected sayings like firmly embedded nails—given by one Shepherd." A goad is a sharp stick a farmer uses to prod his livestock to move in a certain direction. Firmly embedded nails hold things together. The Bible is like a goad—it prods us to action. But like firmly embedded nails, it also holds things together and gives us a firm foundation upon which to build our lives. These words are "given by one Shepherd."

The Bible is like a goad—it prods us to action.

The Lord guided human authors to avoid errors and accurately convey his will to us. Second Peter 1:21 says, "For prophecy never had its origin in the will of man, but men spoke from God as they were carried along by the Holy Spirit." That's why 2 Timothy 3:16,17 says, "All Scripture is God-breathed and is useful for teaching, rebuking, correcting and training in righteousness, so that the man of God may be thoroughly equipped for every good work." This text identifies two positive uses of Scripture (teaching and training) and two negative uses of Scripture (rebuking and correcting).

God gave us Scripture not merely to make us smart, but to make us holy.

God gave us Scripture not merely to make us smart, but to make us holy. That's why Paul says God's Word "is at work in you who believe" (1 Thess 2:13). James 1:22 says, "Do not merely listen to the word, and so deceive yourselves. Do what it says."

‡

C
H
A
P
T
E
R

We need an unquenchable love for God's Word because it tells us about the lives we need to live.

But most of all, we need to have an unquenchable devotion to the Word of God because . . .

It Tells about the Savior We Need to Receive

The Bible is not just a book of rules. It introduces us to the one who forgives us when we've broken the rules. The Bible is not just a list of do's and don'ts. It's the good-news story of the Son of God and his love for us.

> The Bible is not just a book of rules. It introduces us to the one who forgives us when we've broken the rules.

The Old Testament Points to Jesus.

Jesus said, "You diligently study the Scriptures because you think that by them you possess eternal life. These are the Scriptures that testify about me, yet you refuse to come to me to have life. . . . If you believed Moses, you would believe me, for he wrote about me" (John 5:39,40,46).

The Old Testament tells about Christ through prophecies that foretell his coming, through animal sacrifices that point to the cross, through laws that make us aware of God's holiness and our sin, and through the unfolding plan of God to bless all nations through his Son. Jesus said about the Old Testament, "Everything must be fulfilled that is written about me in the Law of Moses, the Prophets, and the Psalms" (Luke 24:44).

> ### Sweet Words
>
> According to an ancient Jewish custom, when a young boy began studying the Scriptures and the Hebrew alphabet, he was given a slate on which to write, and chalk made from a mixture of honey and flour. After a period of instruction, the rabbi would point to the slate; and if the child could identify the words correctly, he was allowed to lick the sweet-tasting letters off the slate as a reward.
>
> The psalmist wrote, "How sweet are your words to my taste, sweeter than honey to my mouth!" (Ps 119:103).

The New Testament Points to Jesus.

In fact, there's so much to tell, the New Testament couldn't even contain everything Jesus said and did. The Bible says, "Jesus did many other things as well. If every one of them were written down, I suppose that even the whole world would not have room for the books that would be written" (John 21:25). John also wrote, "Jesus did many other miraculous signs in the presence of his disciples, which are not recorded in this book. But these are written that you may believe that Jesus is the Christ, the Son of God, and that by believing you may have life in his name" (John 20:30,31).

In 1969, the New York Jets defeated the Baltimore Colts in one of the best-known football games in history. Sports fans remember Super Bowl III for flamboyant quarterback Joe Namath's brash prediction of victory. But students of the game also credit the 16-7 win to some shrewd decisions by Jets' coach Weeb Ewbank. When Ewbank died in November 1998, he still possessed an original handwritten copy of the game plan he followed so successfully 30 years before.

Almost 2,000 years ago, the Lord gave us a game plan, too. God's game plan for the church is recorded in Scripture, with his Son Jesus Christ right in the middle of the action.

Let's develop an unquenchable devotion to God's Word. In a culture gulping down lots of chicken soup for the soul, we'd better make sure the solid meat of God's Word not only appears on the menu, but remains the main course.

> ### Let's develop an unquenchable devotion to God's Word.

---

[1] Alphonse DeLamartine, *Memories of Celebrated Characters*, Vol. 2, 2nd ed. (London: Richard Bentley, 1854) 334.

[2] *The First Epistle of Clement to the Corinthians* (ANF 1:19).

[3] Quoted by Ward Patterson in "A Book Like No Other," *The Lookout*, March 2, 2003.

[4] Mark P. Cosgrove, *The Amazing Body Human: God's Design for Personhood* (Grand Rapids: Baker, 1987) 16.

[5] Cosgrove, *Amazing*, 138-139.

[6] For more information about the historical reliability of the Bible, see my earlier book *Taking Truth Next Door* (Cincinnati: Standard, 1999).

[7] Philip J. King, *Amos, Hosea, Micah—An Archaeological Commentary* (Philadelphia: Westminster, 1988) 144-147.

[8] Associated Press, "Ancient Tablet Echoes Bible Passage," January 13, 2003.

[9] "Is the Bible True?" *U.S. News & World Report*, October 25, 1999.

[10] "Bones of Biblical Family Found," *The Cincinnati Enquirer*, August 15, 1992.

[11] Although the Israel Antiquities Authority has pronounced the James Ossuary a fake, there are many other experts who believe it is of the correct era, whether it is the biblical James or another "Jacob brother of Joshua." See the ongoing reports on this issue in *Biblical Archaeology Review*.

56

✝

C
H
A
P
T
E
R

4   *An Unquenchable Devotion to God's Word*

Developing Unquenchable Faith

1. Do you think of the Bible as God's gift to you? Explain.

2. Tell about a time when the Bible has met your needs in a special way.

3. Have you always believed the Bible is true? If so, why? If not, why not?

4. If a friend asked you to explain why you believe the Bible is God's Word, what would you say?

5. How does the Bible affect your decision-making on a daily basis?

6. Close your time together by having a member of the group read Psalm 119:97-112 as a prayer to the Lord.

Memory Verse
1 Thess 2:13

And we also thank God continually because, when you received the word of God, which you heard from us, you accepted it not as the word of men, but as it actually is, the word of God, which is at work in you who believe.

CHAPTER FIVE

AN UNQUENCHABLE DESIRE TO BUILD UP THE CHURCH

1 THESSALONIANS 2:14–3:13

Some towns have fine-sounding names like Happy Valley, Pennsylvania, and Mount Pleasant, Michigan. Who wouldn't want to live in a place called Paradise Island? What child wouldn't want to live in Santa Claus, Indiana?

And then there's Boring, Oregon. I'm sure Boring has many wonderful assets, but the name must create a public relations challenge for the Boring Chamber of Commerce. Think of all the disgruntled 12-year-olds who have to attend Boring Middle School. An Internet search of the city's Web site tells about Boring businesses and Boring real estate. There's even a Web link called "Boring People."

I was curious. Are there Boring churches, too? Can you imagine trying to invite people to attend "Boring Christian Church"?

Unfortunately, if we are honest, that's the first word that comes to the minds of many people when they hear the word "church." It's boring, or so they think.

On a recent episode of the game show "Family Feud," the host asked the question, "Besides praying, what do people do in church?" One contestant answered, "Sing," and that was indeed one of the answers provided on the survey. Another contestant answered, "Kneel," and again, it was a correct answer according to the survey.

Then another contestant answered, "Read the Bible," and it was *not* a correct answer according to the survey! However, two responses that did appear on the answer board were: "Gossip/talk" and "Sleep." What a sad commentary on the way people see the church!

How do *you* feel about it? Do you love the church? Do you have an unquenchable desire to build up the church?

Of course, "church" doesn't mean a building. It means the *ekklesia*, the called out people of God, rescued from bondage to sin and redeemed by the blood of the Lamb. We don't go to church; we are the church.

Many people today don't like the church very well, and to a certain extent, I understand how they feel. I'm sick of hypocrisy and game-playing in the name of God. I'm tired of "organized religion" that is neither well-organized nor even close to the kind of "pure religion" the Bible talks about—taking care of widows and orphans, living a life of purity and holiness, and keeping our tongues in check (Jas 1:26,27).

I'm weary of churches that have lost their sense of purpose and have become irrelevant, self-centered, and dead.

I'm tired of the way some churches preach about God's love while their members can't even get along among themselves. Or they sing "Amazing Grace," but show an amazing lack of compassion for broken people who need to be loved and restored, not judged and rejected.

I'm tired of seeing Christians divide and quarrel over trivial controversies, while the world around us is going to Hell.

John Heywood (1497–1580) collected a book of English proverbs—the earliest collection of English colloquial sayings. One of his proverbs was, "The nearer to the church, the further from God."

Why Love the Church?

In *The Adventures of Huckleberry Finn*, Mark Twain described a church building that had no lock on the door, and pigs would come in and lie down there because the floor felt cool in the summertime. He said, "If you notice, most folks don't go to church [except] only when they've got to; but a hog is different." Well, I must have something in common with a hog, then, because I can tell you honestly that in spite of its flaws, I love the church, and I want to be filled with a passionate, unquenchable desire to build up the church.

I love the church because Jesus loves the church. Since 1975 I've kept in my office a photograph of my wife Candy—a beautiful picture taken on our wedding day. She's my bride. I'm proud of her. Since the church is the bride of Christ, I love the church.

I love the church because Jesus founded the church. It's his idea, not mine. He said, "On this rock I will build my church, and the gates of Hades will not overcome it" (Matt 16:18). He is the head of the body, the church's one foundation. To say, "I like Jesus, but I don't like the church," is like saying, "I love to swim, but I hate water," or "I like to eat, but I hate food."

I love the church because Jesus gave his life for it. He died on the cross, not merely to save me from my sins as an individual, but to create a body of believers who are clean, radiant, "without stain or wrinkle or any other blemish" (Eph 5:25-27), and so I could live in community with other people who have been saved, forgiven, and empowered by his Spirit. As someone has said, "The church is not made up of people who are better than the rest, but of people who want to become better than they are."

I love the church because the Holy Spirit dwells in it. The church is God's holy temple (1 Cor 3:16,17), his household (1 Tim 3:15), his spiritual dwelling-place (1 Pet 2:4-10).

Near Georgetown, Ohio, is the birthplace of Ulysses S. Grant. One Sunday I preached in Georgetown, and on the way home I stopped and toured the house where Grant lived. It's a simple, unimpressive frame house made of old boards, but a group of visitors listened with interest while a guide told us about every room. The house is important because of the one who lived there. And so it is with the church. "Christ Jesus himself [is] the chief cornerstone. In him the whole building is joined together and rises to become a holy temple in the Lord. And in him you too are being built together to become a dwelling in which God lives by his Spirit" (Eph 2:19-21). Though we are imperfect, God's Spirit lives in us. He dwells among his people. And the spiritual house where he lives isn't just a museum to visit. The church is a busy place—a hospital where people are fed and nurtured back to health, and a training center where we are equipped to serve the King of Kings.

I love the church because the church at its best is a beautiful thing—like the believers in the book of Acts who were "one in heart and mind," who "shared everything they had," who constantly testified about "the resurrection of the Lord Jesus," and of whom the Scripture says, "much grace was upon them all" (Acts 4:32,33).

Remember Boring, Oregon? Guess what I discovered? There's indeed a Christian church in Boring—a growing congregation of over 400 members. It's called "Abundant Life Christian Church."

Church membership means pursuing a God-sized dream that will capture the imagination of present and future followers of Christ. Authentic discipleship is often difficult, but seldom boring. Imagine what can happen when Christians filled with the abundant life of Christ decide to fulfill Jesus' vision of the church. When you make it your passion and your life's goal to build up God's people, your life will not be boring.

An Unquenchable Desire to Build Up the Church

But My Church Has So Many Flaws!

Churches are a mixture of the good and the bad. Eugene Peterson says "the kingdom is equal parts mystery and mess." That shouldn't surprise us. On the positive side, Jesus compared the kingdom of heaven to a buried treasure and a beautiful, priceless pearl (Matt 13:44-46). Yet in the same chapter, Jesus also told the parable of the weeds (Matt 13:24-30), in which he made it plain that on this side of Heaven there will always be a mixture of good and evil within the visible kingdom of God.

Jesus told another parable that made the same point when he spoke about a fishing net that was thrown into the lake and when it was full, the fishermen dragged it up on shore and found it filled with all kinds of fish, both good and bad. Jesus said that's how it will be at the end of time, when God's angels separate the good from the bad (Matt 13:47-50).

It shouldn't surprise us to find some ugliness in the church—a mixture of good and bad, wheat and weeds. The Lord will sort all of that out at the end of time. In the meantime, our job is to build up the church and help it to be the best it can be.

> It shouldn't surprise us to find some ugliness in the church.

If You Decide to Be a Church-Builder

What will happen when you try to build up the Lord's church? What will happen if you have an unquenchable devotion to the family of God? Here are three outcomes you can be sure of: (1) Hardships will test your faith, (2) relationships will give you joy, and (3) God will make you strong.

Hardships Will Test Your Faith

If you're a church builder, you will face *opposition from evildoers.* Jesus said, "If the world hates you, keep in mind that it hated me first" (John 15:18). Paul told the Thessalonians: "For you, brothers, became imitators of God's churches in Judea, which are in Christ Jesus: You suffered from your own countrymen the same things those churches suffered from the Jews, who killed the Lord Jesus and the prophets and also drove us out. They displease God and are hostile to all men in their effort to keep us from speaking to the Gentiles so that they may be saved. In this way they always heap up their sins to the limit. The wrath of God has come upon them at last" (1 Thess 2:14-16). Facing opposition from evildoers is a normal part of the Christian life.

> Facing opposition from evildoers is
> a normal part of the Christian life.

If you're a church builder, you will also face *temptation from Satan.* Paul wrote, "But, brothers, when we were torn away from you for a short time (in person, not in thought), out of our intense longing we made every effort to see you. For we wanted to come to you . . . but Satan stopped us" (2:17,18). He said, "I was afraid that in some way the tempter might have tempted you and our efforts might have been useless" (3:5).

When Paul says "Satan stopped us" (2:18), the word translated "stopped" (Greek *enkopto*) is a strong word that literally means "to cut or strike into." It's a violent picture: an enemy attacking someone and knocking him down or cutting him up. It's a vivid picture of the way Satan tries to stop the church's forward momentum. Some Bible versions say Satan "hindered" or "thwarted" Paul's efforts.

What is Satan doing to hinder you and your church? What temptations are you struggling with right now? When you see a sign that says, "Wet Paint," what makes you want to touch it anyway? The very morning you decide to go on a diet, why does your coworker bring fresh doughnuts to work and place them on your desk? Why do so many marriages break down due to affairs? Why do so many people struggle with addictions?

The Bible says, "Your enemy the devil prowls around like a roaring lion looking for someone to devour." But it also offers us this word of encouragement: "Resist him, standing firm in the faith, because you know that your brothers throughout the world are undergoing the same kind of sufferings" (1 Pet 5:8,9).

Temptation is real, but we are not defenseless.

Temptation is real, but we are not defenseless. "No temptation has seized you except what is common to man. And God is faithful; he will not let you be tempted beyond what you can bear. But when you are tempted, he will also provide a way out so that you can stand up under it" (1 Cor 10:13).

SATAN'S SCHEMES AGAINST THE CHURCH

The apostle Paul warned that Satan "masquerades as an angel of light" and tries to lead Christians astray from our "sincere and pure devotion to Christ" (2 Cor 11:3,14). Yet, in a healthy church filled with faith and forgiveness, the devil will "not outwit us. For we are not unaware of his schemes" (2 Cor 2:11).

What are some of the devil's schemes? The book of Acts reveals several ways he tried to disrupt the New Testament church:

Through greed and dishonesty. Satan moved Ananias and Sapphira to lie to the Holy Spirit and keep back money from some property they sold (Acts 5:3).

By trying to prevent seekers from hearing and believing the gospel. When a government ruler named Sergius Paulus wanted to hear the Word of God, a sorcerer named Elymas tried to prevent him from believing in the Lord. Paul looked at him and said, "You are a child of the devil and an enemy of everything that is right! You are full of all kinds of deceit and trickery" (Acts 13:6-12).

By deceiving people through false wonders. In Philippi, Paul and Silas met a slave girl who predicted the future with the help of an evil spirit. She must have been good at it, because "she earned a great deal of money for her owners by fortune-telling." Paul cast the demon out of her, and the owners of the slave girl became angry because their means of making money was gone (Acts 16:16-18). Satan sometimes displays his power through "all kinds of counterfeit miracles, signs and wonders" (2 Thess 2:9).

Satan worked behind the scenes in other ways as well:

- Stirring up violence and persecution against Christians (Acts 7:54–8:3; 12:1-4);
- Planting seeds of pride and greed in the heart of Simon the sorcerer in Samaria, who wanted to "buy the gift of God with money" (Acts 8:9-24);
- Enslaving people through the indwelling of evil spirits (Acts 19:11-16).

Yet, the New Testament church emerged victorious, for the Christians followed Jesus who "went around doing good and healing all who were under the power of the devil" (Acts 10:38). The Son of God came "to destroy the devil's work" (1 John 3:8).

Furthermore, if you are a church builder, *you will face persecution from the world.* Paul warned the Thessalonians not to "be unsettled by these trials" they would face. "In fact, when we were with you," Paul continued, "we kept telling you that we would be persecuted. And it turned out that way, as you well know" (3:3,4).

But there are also a number of very positive things that will happen when you build up the church.

Relationships Will Give You Joy

The apostle Paul asked, "For what is our hope, our joy, or the crown in which we will glory in the presence of our Lord Jesus when he comes? Is it not you? Indeed, you are our glory and joy" (2:19,20). Relationships with other Christians filled Paul's heart with joy. Later he exclaimed, "How can we thank God enough for you in return for all the joy we have in the presence of our God because of you?" (3:9).

Have you ever experienced the wonderful satisfaction that comes from working closely and productively with a like-minded brother or sister in Christ? Paul found this kind of joy in the close working relationship he shared with his friend Timothy. He said, "We sent Timothy, who is our brother and God's fellow worker in spreading the gospel of Christ, to strengthen and encourage you in your faith" (3:2). And Paul rejoiced when Timothy brought good news about the condition of the

Thessalonian church: "But Timothy has just now come to us from you and has brought good news about your faith and love. He has told us that you always have pleasant memories of us and that you long to see us, just as we also long to see you. Therefore, brothers, in all our distress and persecution we were encouraged about you because of your faith. For *now we really live*, since you are standing firm in the Lord" (3:7,8, emphasis mine).

What makes you really come alive? Paul says, "now we really live." But when? When we give ourselves to the work of the Lord! "Now we really live"—when we help other Christians grow. "Now we really live"—when the faithful examples of other Christians inspire us to serve the Lord.

I was asked to preach at a church in Alabama. Before the worship service began, I was invited to attend an adult Bible class. In the first few minutes of the class time, the class members were drinking coffee and eating some breakfast snacks someone had brought in. I sat next to a fellow named Jerry who, it turned out, is a medical doctor.

The class leader began to take prayer requests from the group and write them on the white-board in front of the room. Someone asked for prayer for those serving in our nation's military forces, and for the President. Someone else mentioned a little child who was suffering in the hospital. Others mentioned the death of a parent, concerns for their grown children who lived in another country, and a variety of other requests. I thought to myself, "This is so important—to have others around to support you."

Just then Jerry leaned over and pointed to a man sitting in the back of the room. He whispered, "See that guy back there?" I nodded. He said, "That guy gave me his kidney."

I must have looked puzzled, so Jerry continued. "Yeah, I was sick a couple of years ago and I needed a kidney transplant." It turns out that these two men were not related, and they had no other connection except they were members of the same church and had compatible blood types. Jerry's friend at church gave him a kidney. "Now we really live"—when we see Christians exercising brotherly love in such a sacrificial, inspiring way.

When you build up the Lord's church, hardships will test your faith. Relationships will give you joy. And . . .

God Will Make You Strong

Paul prayed for the Thessalonians, "May the Lord make your love increase and overflow for each other and for everyone else, just as ours does for you. May he strengthen your hearts so that you will be blameless

An Unquenchable Desire to Build Up the Church 5

and holy in the presence of our God and Father when our Lord Jesus comes with all his holy ones" (3:12,13).

God loves you just as you are, but he loves you too much to leave you as you are. He is calling you into fellowship with others so that your love will increase. As you worship and serve him shoulder to shoulder with other believers, he will strengthen your heart. He will keep spurring you on toward greater holiness and godliness until his Son comes again.

So even though you see imperfections in the church, don't give up on it. Be a church builder. Ask God to give you an unquenchable love for the body of Christ. Do your part to build up the church. Instead of finding fault with your congregation, find ways to make it better. Make it your goal to agree with Jonathan Edwards who said, "Resolved: that all men should live for the glory of God. Resolved second: that whether others do or not, I will."

> Even though you see imperfections in the church, don't give up on it. Be a church builder.

5   *An Unquenchable Desire to Build Up the Church*

Developing Unquenchable Faith

1. Be honest. How do you really feel about the church? What do you love about it? What bothers you about it?

2. The Bible makes it clear that Christians will face temptation and even persecution. What temptations are you wrestling with right now? How is Satan trying to hinder God's work in your life?

3. The apostle Paul wrote, "For now we really live, since you are standing firm in the Lord" (1 Thess 3:8). Why do you think he found so much joy in the spiritual progress of others? Tell about a time when you have experienced that same sense of satisfaction.

4. Brainstorm about some practical ways your group can build up your local church. What can you do to help your congregation reach its full potential? Decide on at least one action step you will undertake as a group.

5. Close your group by praying for your church—its unity, its effectiveness, its growth, and health.

> **Memory Verse**
> 1 Thess 1:19-20
>
> *For what is our hope, our joy, or the crown in which we will glory in the presence of our Lord Jesus when he comes? Is it not you? Indeed, you are our glory and joy.*

CHAPTER SIX

AN UNQUENCHABLE COMMITMENT TO SEXUAL PURITY

1 THESSALONIANS 4:1-12

A cartoon shows a young man talking to his grandfather. The young fellow says, "Granddad, your generation didn't have all these social diseases. What did you wear to have safe sex?" And the grandfather replies, "A wedding ring."

God created us to be sexual beings. In the Garden of Eden he created Adam and Eve, and they were "naked and not ashamed." God told them to be fruitful and multiply, but even animals can multiply. For people created in his image, God intended sex to be an enjoyable expression of physical, emotional, and spiritual love.

Sex is intertwined with intimacy, which is why the Old Testament sometimes talks about sexual relations by saying a man "knew" his wife and she became pregnant. Sex is far more than just a physical act. It's a holy sharing of two lives. It's knowing each other deeply, within the security of a lifetime commitment.

As long as it's not misused, sex has God's blessing. It is a beautiful gift to be enjoyed within the bounds of marriage. Scripture tells husbands, "Rejoice in the wife of your youth . . . may you ever be captivated by her love" (Prov 5:18,19). A whole book of the Bible, Song of Solomon, is a romantic poem portraying the tender affection between a husband and his wife. In 1 Corinthians 7, the apostle Paul encourages husbands and wives to meet each other's sexual needs.

> As long as it's not misused, sex has God's blessing.

But sex is like fire. Keep it inside the fireplace, and it warms your house. Let it rage out of control, and people get hurt. Sex is like a river. Keep it inside its banks, and it's beautiful and refreshing. But when it floods its banks, it leaves destruction in its wake. Instead of staying within its God-given boundaries, today sex is being misused and is causing great harm.

Today sex is being misused and is causing great harm.

- At least one out of five adult women and one out of 10 adult men report having been sexually abused in childhood. In America, child sexual abuse is reported as many as 80,000 times per year, and it's likely the number of unreported instances is far greater.[1]
- In a typical month, three million American young people under age 17 visit an adult web site on their computers.[2]
- Sexual sins condemned in the Bible are routine subjects of TV shows, movies, and comedy routines.

Someone has described today's world as a "zero-morality environment." It's like a zero-gravity environment where there is nothing to hold onto, nothing to keep you from floating this way and that. But we do have something to hold onto—the Lord and his Word. This is not a time for Christians to give up. It's a time for Christians to demonstrate a positive and unquenchable commitment to sexual purity.

It Starts in Your Heart

The apostle Paul begins First Thessalonians chapter 4 by saying, "Finally, brothers, we instructed you how to live in order to please God, *as in fact you are living. Now we ask you and urge you in the Lord Jesus to do this more and more*" (v. 1, emphasis mine). Notice, he is not writing these things to shame his brethren, but to remind and encourage them to put into practice the truth they already know.

The exhortations that follow are not merely the musings of an uninspired moralist. Paul reminds the Thessalonians, "For you know what instructions we gave you by the authority of the Lord Jesus" (v. 2). The full force of the authority of Christ himself undergirds the instructions given by the inspired apostles.

Jesus made it clear that sexual purity starts in our hearts. He taught, "You have heard that it was said, 'Do not commit adultery.' But I tell you that anyone who looks at a woman lustfully has already committed adultery with her in his heart" (Matt 5:27,28). Another time he said, "For out of the heart come evil thoughts, murder, adultery, [and] sexual immorality" (Matt 15:19).

69

‡

C
H
A
P
T
E
R

An Unquenchable Commitment to Sexual Purity **6**

When Candy and I started dating, I couldn't take my eyes off her. I keep pictures of her in my wallet and in my office. When she walks into a room, my eyes light up. I'm glad God made her good looking! The Bible tells us that Sarah, Rebekah, and Abigail were very beautiful, and David was handsome. It's not wrong to notice and appreciate someone's good looks. But deep in our hearts we know when we've crossed the line from healthy admiration to sinful lust.

> It's not wrong to appreciate beauty, but deep in our hearts we know when we've crossed the line.

The Harm Caused by Sexual Sin

We do not have to wonder about God's will in these matters. Paul plainly states, "It is God's will that you should be sanctified: that you should avoid sexual immorality; that each of you should learn to control his own body in a way that is holy and honorable, not in passionate lust like the heathen, who do not know God" (vv. 3-5). There should be a noticeable difference in the sexual behavior of Christians, in marked contrast with those "who do not know God" and whose lives are characterized by uncontrolled "passionate lust."

The Christians in Thessalonica faced a great deal of sexual temptation. In first-century Greek culture, marital faithfulness "was regarded as an unreasonable demand on a man. In society at large it was taken for granted that men would naturally seek the satisfaction of their sexual desires outside the marriage bond."[3] Yet, Paul insisted that the church should not conform to the loose sexual standards of its surrounding culture.

Sexual purity is a difficult challenge for us today. Job said, "I have made a covenant with my eyes not to look lustfully at a girl" (Job 31:1), but such a covenant is harder to keep if you have a computer in your home or office and temptation is only a few clicks away. With so much pornography on the Internet, the anonymity factor has gone way up, the accountability factor has gone way down, sexual addictions are escalating, and women are being devalued. Online affairs are a growing problem because computer users in e-mail chat rooms are getting involved in online relationships that go at microwave speed. Pornography is a cheap substitute for real intimacy.

Sexual sin is harmful on many levels.

- *It damages others.* "In this matter no one should wrong his brother or take advantage of him" (1 Thess 4:6). True love "is not self-seeking" (1 Cor 13:5).

An Unquenchable Commitment to Sexual Purity

- *It damages our relationship with God.* "The Lord will punish men for all such sins, as we have already told you and warned you" (1 Thess 4:6). This is serious business. "Marriage should be honored by all, and the marriage bed kept pure, for God will judge the adulterer and all the sexually immoral" (Heb 13:5).
- *It damages our bodies and our emotions.* "Flee from sexual immorality. All other sins a man commits are outside his body, but he who sins sexually sins against his own body" (1 Cor 6:18). Physically, promiscuity carries with it the danger of sexually transmitted disease. Emotionally, it scars the conscience and damages the heart. Lewis Smedes observed, "We cannot take our bodies to bed with someone and park our souls outside in the car to wait."

> **"We cannot take our bodies to bed with someone and park our souls outside in the car to wait."**

- *It damages our testimony to a watching world.* "For God did not call us to be impure, but to live a holy life" (1 Thess 4:7). Unholy living weakens our witness. "Dear friends, I urge you, as aliens and strangers in the world, to abstain from sinful desires, which war against your soul. Live such good lives among the pagans that, though they accuse you of doing wrong, they may see your good deeds and glorify God on the day he visits us" (1 Pet 2:11,12).
- *It dishonors the Lord.* "He who rejects this instruction does not reject man but God, who gives you the Holy Spirit" (1 Thess 4:8).

The Lord's Plan for Marriage

According to Matthew chapter 19, some Pharisees came to Jesus and asked him, "Is it lawful for a man to divorce his wife for any and every reason?" From the tone of their question, it sounds like they were more interested in finding a way out than a way to stay in. Jesus responded by explaining God's plan for marriage.

God's plan for marriage is revealed in Scripture. Jesus asked, "Haven't you read . . . ?" (Matt 19:4), then he quoted from the book of Genesis about God's creation of Adam and Eve. Our thoughts about marriage need to be guided by God's Word, not merely by our own feelings, our cultural norms, or the opinions of our friends. We need to get our ideas about marriage from the Bible, not from movie stars and TV talk-show hosts.

> **We need to get our ideas about marriage from the Bible, not from movie stars and TV talk-show hosts.**

An Unquenchable Commitment to Sexual Purity

God's plan for marriage reflects the way we were created. "In the beginning the Creator made them," Jesus said (Matt 19:4). Our sexuality isn't an insignificant part of us. It's deeply connected to who we are inside, and what we were designed to be.

> **According to Jesus, there's no such thing as a "same-sex marriage."**

God's plan for marriage requires a man and a woman. God "made them male and female" (Matt 19:4; Gen 1:27). According to Jesus, there's no such thing as a "same-sex marriage," for marriage requires a male and a female. This basic truth echoes throughout the Bible. Leviticus 18:22 says, "Do not lie with a man as one lies with a woman; that is detestable." Romans chapter 1 refers to homosexual behavior with words like "shameful," "degrading," "indecent," and "unnatural." First Corinthians 6:9 says "the wicked will not inherit the kingdom of God"—including the sexually immoral, idolaters, adulterers, male prostitutes, homosexual offenders, thieves, the greedy, drunkards, and swindlers. "And that is what some of you were," the Bible says. "But you were washed, you were sanctified, you were justified in the name of the Lord Jesus Christ and by the Spirit of our God" (1 Cor 6:11).

In Christ, there's always hope, grace, and forgiveness. God loves us no matter what temptations and struggles we face. But no matter how much the world tells us otherwise, homosexual behavior is not acceptable to God.

God's plan for marriage requires a clear commitment. Jesus said, "'For this reason a man will leave his father and mother and be united to his wife, and the two will become one flesh'" (Matt 19:5; Gen 2:24). Wedding customs vary from one culture to another, but marriage always involves a public commitment—a time when husband and wife make it clear they are leaving their parents' homes to establish a life-long bond with each other.

Have you ever heard someone say that a marriage license is "just a piece of paper"? Actually, some pieces of paper are very important—like paychecks, diplomas, property deeds, and letters from close friends. A marriage license is important. But the real issue is not the license, but what we believe about marriage itself.

- Marriage *is not* buying a car, where you test-drive it first and trade it for a different model if you decide you don't like it.
- Marriage *is not* a chemistry experiment, where you casually combine different elements and hope they don't explode.
- Marriage *is not* a game, where you bluff, tease, maneuver, and compete.

An Unquenchable Commitment to Sexual Purity

- Marriage *is not* an antique—a quaint, fragile leftover from a bygone era.
- Marriage *is not* a constant party, but neither is it a grim prison sentence.

God sees marriage as a covenant promise—a holy mystery that pictures the relationship between Christ and his church (see Eph 5:21-33). In God's eyes, marriage means cherishing your partner in sickness and health, wealth and poverty, periods of depression and times of joy. Marriage means "loving your neighbor" in the give-and-take of daily living.

WHAT ABOUT "LIVING TOGETHER"?

In America in 1960, about 400,000 couples were living together without being married. Today that number has grown to over four million. Some couples cohabit because they've watched their parents' marriages break up, and they're cautious about committing to marriage. Others do it for economic reasons, so they don't have to pay for two separate residences.

There are several good reasons, though, *not* to live together before marriage:

(1) *It's scripturally wrong.* No matter what the world says about it, or how acceptable cohabitation has become in our culture, it violates God's standards of sexual purity to sleep with someone who is not your spouse.

(2) *It's statistically indefensible.* After studying 50 years of data, researchers at Brigham Young University found that couples who live together before marriage have a 50 percent greater likelihood of getting a divorce than those who don't live together prior to marriage. Actually, out of every five couples who live together before marriage, four do not stay together. Two out of five break up before they marry. Another two out of five divorce within 10 years of marriage.

(3) *It's emotionally hazardous.* How secure can you feel with a partner who wants to sleep with you without marrying you? Why should you share the most intimate part of yourself with someone who won't first promise his faithfulness for life? A Rutgers University study found that couples who live together before marriage score lower than other married couples in most areas of well-being, including sexual satisfaction. Cohabiting partners typically experience higher levels of unfaithfulness, conflict, and domestic violence than married couples.

(4) *It's economically unjustifiable.* If it's morally wrong, it's not okay just because it will save money to share one house or apartment. If an unmarried couple sincerely want to do the right thing in God's eyes, most churches will do their best to help them find alternative housing arrangements.

(5) *It's harmful to kids.* Children need a dad and a mom, not a live-in companion who may be gone next month. When our young children grow up and become teenagers and young adults, we need every ounce of moral authority we can muster to help them see why they shouldn't engage in premarital sex. Do the right thing for your kids: Don't live together until you're married!

Jesus not only tells us what we *shouldn't* do; he also tells us about the positive side. His message isn't just, "Don't live together before marriage." The Lord wants couples to really LIVE together AFTER marriage! Jesus said a husband and wife are "united" or "joined together" by God (Matt 19:6). In marriage two lives merge as one, creating a unique and positive synergy. The Lord wants couples to have a happy, healthy, enjoyable, Christ-honoring, fulfilling marriage. That takes preparation and hard work, but it beats the pain that occurs when a marriage falls apart.

> His message isn't just, "Don't live together before marriage." The Lord wants couples to really LIVE together AFTER marriage!

Practical Steps toward Sexual Purity

God's "commands are not burdensome" (1 John 5:3); they are for our own good. So what can we do to encourage sexual purity in our personal lives, in our families, and in our churches?

74 What the Church Can Do

The church can emphasize preparation for marriage through engaged couples classes and quality pastoral counseling before couples marry. The church can also encourage preservation of marriage by helping couples discover "positive fidelity"—positive reasons to stay together and enjoy their relationship.

We need to hold one another accountable. Men's groups can offer practical help for those struggling to rid their lives of pornography. If you see a brother or sister slipping into a sexual danger zone, talk with them. Don't just shrug your shoulders when you hear about friends who are struggling in their marriage or someone who's having an affair. Love them enough to pray for them and encourage them to persevere in their marriage.

We need to hold one another accountable.

In the church we also need to minister redemptively with those whose lives have been touched by divorce. Doesn't the Bible say God hates divorce? Yes (see Malachi 1:16). But it doesn't say he hates divorced *people*. The Bible says of Jesus, "a bruised reed he will not break, and a smoldering wick he will not snuff out" (Matt 12:20). The Lord didn't come to crush people who are already bruised, already burning out. He came to restore us and put the pieces back together.

If you did all you could, but your marriage fell apart . . . if a former spouse left you broken and burned . . . if you look back with regret on your own part in a marriage breakup . . . God's grace is still sufficient for you. The reason God allowed divorce in the first place was to protect women from being harmed by hard-hearted men (see Deut 24:1-4, Matt 19:7-9). If you have been divorced, you aren't a second-class citizen in the kingdom of God. God's grace is abundant and free, and the church should be a place of healing, forgiveness, and growth. Wise churches sponsor divorce recovery groups and programs for single parents.

When "the saints go marchin' in," they don't all march in pairs!

And speaking of singles—we need to remember that singleness is noble in God's eyes. When "the saints go marchin' in," they don't all march in pairs! More than one-third of all the adults in America are either widowed, divorced, separated, or have never been married. All of us who are married were single at one time, and we'll be single again if our spouse precedes us in death.

Jesus was single. So was the apostle Paul. If you choose to remain single, God is satisfied with your choice too. Sometimes "it is better not to marry" (see Matt 19:10-12, 1 Cor 7:1-40). Some of us can serve God more effectively if we remain single instead of getting married. All over the world, singles are serving the Lord, reaching the lost, embracing the lonely, and making a difference for Jesus Christ. Singles need to be included in our fellowship and valued in the church. We need to offer them hospitality and include them in our prayers.

An Unquenchable Commitment to Sexual Purity

What We Can Do as Individuals

If you've committed sexual sin, confess it to God and seek help. First John 1:9 says, "If we confess our sins, he is faithful and just and will forgive us our sins and purify us from all unrighteousness." James 5:16 says, "Therefore confess your sins to each other and pray for each other so that you may be healed. The prayer of a righteous man is powerful and effective." Find one or two trustworthy Christian friends who will hold you accountable and help you be victorious in your struggle for sexual purity.

If you're going to marry, prepare for it spiritually. Don't be impulsive and make a foolish choice. Next to becoming a Christian, the decision to marry is likely to be the biggest decision you'll ever make. Bathe the process in prayer. Seek wise counsel. Get involved in an engaged couples class or in premarital counseling. Benjamin Franklin said, "Keep your eyes wide open before marriage, and half shut afterward."

If you have already committed to marriage, preserve and protect it. Don't view marriage as a ball and chain that takes away your freedom. Keep growing together. Even if your marriage is struggling, God can restore you and strengthen your relationship.

> **If your marriage is hurting, see how much music you can still make with what you have left.**

One evening, as the violinist Itzhak Perlman gave a concert in New York City, one of his violin strings broke with a loud snap. Perlman continued to play, improvising on the three remaining strings. The crowd cheered when he finished, and later Perlman said, "You know, sometimes it is the artist's task to find out how much music you can still make with what you have left." If your marriage is hurting, see how much music you can still make with what you have left.

A Lifestyle of Love

Preoccupied with the sensual, today's world highlights sexuality, but the Bible also talks about many other dimensions of love. First Thessalonians 4:9-12 emphasizes that a Christian's daily activity should exemplify a lifestyle of love.

THE EXAMPLE OF LOVE: *"Now about brotherly love we do not need to write to you, for you yourselves have been taught by God to love each other"* (v. 9). The Lord himself teaches us to love. "This is how we know what love is: Jesus Christ laid down his life for us. And we ought to lay down our lives for our brothers" (1 John 3:16).

An Unquenchable Commitment to Sexual Purity

> **THE EXTENT OF LOVE**: *"And in fact, you do love all the brothers throughout Macedonia. Yet we urge you, brothers, to do so more and more"* (v. 10). We can never say we've fully arrived, for no matter how much we love others, we can still "do so more and more."
>
> **THE PRACTICAL IMPACT OF LOVE**: *"Make it your ambition to lead a quiet life, to mind your own business and to work with your hands, just as we told you"* (v. 11). We demonstrate love in practical ways by avoiding gossip and by living well-ordered, disciplined lives characterized by hard work.
>
> **THE POSITIVE OUTCOME OF LOVE**: *"So that your daily life may win the respect of outsiders and so that you will not be dependent on anybody"* (v. 12).

What Our Families Can Do

"Fathers, do not exasperate your children; instead, bring them up in the training and instruction of the Lord" (Eph 6:4). This includes instruction about sexual purity.

If you're a parent, model healthy, biblical attitudes about sexual purity. Monitor your child's TV habits and computer use. Set a good example in your own lifestyle. Talk to your children and help them say "no" to sexual pressure. Remind them that waiting until marriage will protect them from sexually transmitted diseases. It will protect them from emotional harm. It will build their self-esteem and develop their trust in God. It will protect them from painful memories and increase their joy in marriage.

Most of all, remind them that waiting until marriage will honor the Lord.

A woman sent a little poem to Ann Landers that went like this: *I met him. I liked him. I loved him. I let him. I lost him.* Later a man sent a different poem to Ann Landers, which went like this: *I saw her. I liked her. I loved her. I wanted her. I asked her. She said no. I married her. After 60 years, I still have her.*

With God's help, we can win the battle for sexual purity if we make it the unquenchable commitment of our hearts.

---

[1] American Academy of Child and Adolescent Psychiatry, *Report on Child Sexual Abuse*, November, 1998.

[2] *Business Wire*, December 19, 2000.

[3] Leon Morris, *The First and Second Epistles to the Thessalonians* (Grand Rapids: Eerdmans, 1959) 121.

An Unquenchable Commitment to Sexual Purity

Developing Unquenchable Faith

1. What does the word "family" mean to you? Does "family" bring mostly positive or negative thoughts and feelings to you?

2. Why do you think sexual purity is such a struggle for so many of us today?

3. What can your group do to encourage sexual purity in your individual hearts? In your marriages? In the lives of your children (and/or grandchildren)? In your community?

4. First Thessalonians 4:7 says, "For God did not call us to be impure, but to live a holy life." Sexual impurity is only one kind of sin, and other sins make us "impure" before God as well. In the larger sense, what does it mean to "live a holy life"?

5. Close the group session with a time of prayer. Encourage each member of the group to silently confess to God any impurity in his or her heart. Close by reading aloud David's prayer of confession recorded in Psalm 51:1-12.

Memory Verse
1 Thess 4:3-4

It is God's will that you should be holy; that you should avoid sexual immorality; that each of you should learn to control his own body in a way that is holy and honorable.

CHAPTER SEVEN

UNQUENCHABLE HOPE FOR THE FUTURE

1 THESSALONIANS 4:13-18

A soldier in the Middle East lies down at night and pulls out a picture of his wife and two-year-old daughter. He prays for them and looks forward to holding them in his arms again. He keeps going because of hope.

A student stays up late working on a research paper for class. Graduation seems far away, but she keeps going because of hope.

An elderly man has been in the hospital for weeks. His back aches from lying in bed so long, and his arms are bruised from blood tests and IVs. The doctors tell him if he keeps making progress he might be home in time for Easter, so he keeps going because of hope.

A widow visits her husband's grave. She remembers all those years they spent together bringing up children, working, and saving for retirement. Then a heart attack suddenly took him away, and she misses him so much that some days she wonders how she can go on. As her finger traces the phrase carved on her husband's tombstone, the words give her a strange sensation of peace. The engraving says, "Till we meet again." She keeps going because of hope.

We need hope like a fish needs water, like a flower needs the sun. Our spirits need hope like our lungs need air and our stomachs need food.

> We need hope like a fish needs water, like a flower needs the sun.

Mark Jones tells about a town that was located near a river, and government officials decided to build a dam so the river would become a lake. This meant the town would be covered with water. Once the decision was made to destroy the town, it began to change. Buildings that used to be beautiful began to deteriorate. Well-kept yards became overgrown with weeds. Paint faded and peeled from the houses. Why bother to maintain your property if you knew it would soon be at the bottom of a lake? Likewise, Mark says, "When there is no hope for the future, the present becomes empty and meaningless."[1]

Our possessions can't give us hope. There's a car called an "Infiniti." It's a very nice car. But do you know where that Infiniti is going to be in 30 years? In a junkyard covered with rust. It's not really infinite. Go to a sporting goods store and you can buy equipment made by a company called "EverLast." It's good quality, but it won't last forever. The baseball Mark McGwire hit for his record-setting 70th home run sold for more than $3 million. Imagine paying such a huge sum for a ball that will sit on a shelf! But all of the things money can buy are like the way a baseball announcer describes a home run—"going, going, gone!"

Non-Christian religions can't give us hope. Hinduism sticks its adherents into a futile cycle of reincarnation. Buddhism doesn't offer a personal relationship with a risen Savior. Islam and Judaism teach there is one true God, but they don't solve the problem of sin or give assurance of eternal life.

Astrology can't give us hope. When a TV psychic network declared bankruptcy, its lawyer declared, "They made some bad decisions due to unforeseen circumstances." (Perhaps they should have seen it coming.)

Despite all the good they do, *science and technology can't give us hope.* The finest physician cannot prolong our lives forever. The earth's resources are not infinite. As one science reporter noted with a touch of melancholy, eventually "the stars will simply wink out—and the universe will end, not with a bang but with the mildest of whimpers."

By themselves, *other people can't give us hope.* Thurman Munson was an All-Star catcher for the New York Yankees. He died in a plane crash in 1979. Yankees owner George Steinbrenner said at the time, "Thurman Munson was our rock, the fortress—invincible. Baseball is just a tiny little speck when something like this hits home."

> **We can't live without hope and without God.**
> **When we try to do so, we feel miserable.**

We can't live without hope. And as we face the future, the only "rock" and "fortress" who offers invincible hope is Jesus Christ. That's why in 1 Thessalonians 4:13 the apostle Paul says, "Brothers, we do not want you to be ignorant about those who fall asleep, or to grieve

Unquenchable Hope for the Future

like the rest of men, who have no hope" (v. 13). Ephesians 2:12 says that when we're lost in sin we're "without hope and without God in the world." We can't live without hope and without God. When we try to do so, we feel miserable. God wants to give us an unquenchable hope. In fact, hope is one of the great themes of the Bible.

When Adam and Eve sinned, death, pain, and sorrow entered the world. But God promised that someday the "seed of woman" would crush the serpent's head (Gen 3:15). There was hope.

David wrote in the Psalms, "Find rest, O my soul, in God alone; my hope comes from him" (Ps 62:5).

Isaiah said that those who "hope in the Lord will renew their strength" (Isa 40:31).

> ### The Bible calls God "the God of hope."

The Bible calls God "the God of hope" (Rom 15:13). Hebrews 6:19 calls hope "an anchor for the soul, firm and secure." Paul told Titus we are waiting "for the blessed hope—the glorious appearing of our great God and Savior, Jesus Christ" (Titus 2:13).

In an earlier part of his letter to the Thessalonians, Paul said he wanted to come and supply what was lacking in their faith (3:10). Evidently one area where their understanding was still lacking involved the circumstances of Christians who had already died, and the promised reality of Jesus' future return. God doesn't want us to be ignorant about these matters. Every chapter of 1 Thessalonians ends with a reference to the return of Christ. What does 1 Thessalonians chapter 4 tell us about our hope?

Our Hope Is Grounded in Solid Facts

Paul writes, "We believe that Jesus died and rose again" (v. 14). The death, burial, and resurrection of Christ are historical realities, not pipe dreams. As professor Leon Morris has stated, "The resurrection is the great triumphant act wherein the divine quality of the Christian gospel is conclusively demonstrated."[2] God "has given us new birth into a living hope through the resurrection of Jesus Christ from the dead" (1 Pet 1:3).

> ### The death, burial, and resurrection of Christ are historical realities, not pipe dreams.

When Candy and I visited the Holy Land, on a gorgeous spring day we visited the Garden Tomb in Jerusalem. There's no way to be sure the Garden Tomb is the actual site of Jesus' resurrection, but it fits the description well. The tomb is cut out of solid rock, with a large groove in front so a stone could be rolled across the entrance. There's even a large crack in the side of the cliff—earthquake damage, the guide told us.

After we were there a while and had taken some pictures, I stepped into the tomb by myself. There on the right side of the entrance was a ledge carved out of the rock, designed to hold a body. It was an incredibly moving moment—to think I might be standing in the very place where Jesus rose from the dead.

I thought, "Thank God, Jesus' body isn't here. The tomb is empty!" But then it dawned on me. Right at that moment, it *wasn't* empty, because I was there. And I was there 2,000 years ago too. I was on Jesus' mind and in his heart when he died on Calvary. When I accepted Christ by faith and was baptized into him, I was united with him in his death and resurrection (Rom 6:1-4).

Jesus died and his body was sealed in a garden tomb. But three days later, he was alive again—teaching, eating, interacting with his disciples, giving them 40 days' worth of evidence that his resurrection was a fact (Acts 1:3). His resurrection wasn't a myth. Over 500 people saw him (1 Cor 15:6).

In the 1960s Jerry Lee Lewis sang, "There's a whole lot of shakin' going on!" On Jesus' resurrection day, there was a whole lot of shakin' going on. *The ground shook* (Matt 28:2), just as it did a few days earlier when Jesus died on the cross. Also, *the guards shook*. These were seasoned soldiers. Normally they weren't afraid of anything, but when an angel appeared as bright as lightning, wearing clothes that shone like the sun on new-fallen snow, the guards trembled with fear (Matt 28:3,4). God was shaking things up! Yet, the angel of the Lord "rolled back the stone and *sat on it*" (Matt 28:2)—calm, cool, and confident because God was in control.

> **We all know what it's like to be shaken up.**

We all know what it's like to be shaken up. A doctor tells us bad news. The stock market dips and dives. War takes the lives of young soldiers. Like the women who came to Jesus' tomb early on Sunday morning, we're all "looking for Jesus, who was crucified" (Matt 28:5). We're all headed for the tomb, searching in the dim light of dawn for a reason to hope. And then to our surprise, we find God has already been at work. We all need to hear the wonderful news that "he has risen, just as he said" (Matthew 28:6).

Our Hope Is Grounded in the Promises of Jesus Himself

The promised hope we embrace is "according to the Lord's own word" (1 Thess 4:15). Five times in three verses (vv. 15,16,17) Paul calls Jesus "the Lord." Christ is the ultimate authority. His words carry enormous weight. The fact of Jesus' coming is not just Paul's opinion. It's not just speculation. Jesus himself promised to go and prepare a place for us. He promised to come again and receive us unto himself (John 14:1-3). He promised to be with us always (Matt 28:20).

> **Christ is the ultimate authority.
> His words carry enormous weight.**

Joshua 23:14 says, "You know with all your heart and soul that not one of all the good promises the Lord your God gave you has failed. Every promise has been fulfilled; not one has failed" (Joshua 23:14).

Jim and Elaine Hutchison minister with Bedford Acres Christian Church near Lexington, Kentucky. Several years ago Elaine's first husband David was driving to church on a Sunday evening when a car ran a stop sign and hit his car broadside. Elaine and her young daughter witnessed the accident, and David died in Elaine's arms. She was nine months pregnant at the time—a widow at the age of 27.

In the midst of her grief, someone gave Elaine a plaque that read, "Lord, there's nothing that's going to happen to me today that you and I can't handle together." That became her motto.

A few weeks later and hundreds of miles away, Jim Hutchison's wife Vivian went into the hospital for routine surgery, but she didn't come out of the anesthesia as she should. Two weeks later she died, and Jim was left to raise two little boys, ages two and four, by himself. Jim says before his wife died, he never heard his boys stir during the night. After she died, he heard every move they made.

Eventually the widower Jim met the widow Elaine. They married and raised their children together. When I asked them how they made it through, Jim said, "We practiced the old cliché—take things one day at a time. And when you can't do that, take it an hour at a time." But the bigger thing Jim said that helped was a verse of Scripture. In Jeremiah 29:11 the Lord says, "I know the plans I have for you, plans to prosper you and not to harm you, plans to give you hope and a future."

Without Christ, life is a hopeless end; with Christ, it's an endless hope. When we know Jesus as our Savior and Lord, we have "crossed over from death to life" (John 5:24). God's promises give us a calm assurance.

83

‡

C
H
A
P
T
E
R

Our Hope Looks Forward to the Return of Christ

Paul writes, "We tell you that we who are still alive, who are left till the coming of the Lord, will certainly not precede those who have fallen asleep. For the Lord himself will come down from heaven" (v. 16).

There's a lot I don't know about the return of Christ. I don't know when he will come. I don't know exactly how he will come. But I do know who is coming!

> **I don't know when or how he will come,
> but I do know who is coming!**

After Jesus ascended into heaven, the angels said, "Men of Galilee, why do you stand here looking into the sky? This same Jesus, who has been taken from you into heaven, will come back in the same way you have seen him go into heaven" (Acts 1:11).

The early church had such an unquenchable expectation of the Lord's return, they had a special prayer, the Aramaic *Marana tha*, which means "Come, O Lord" (1 Cor 16:22).

The Bible ends with the apostle John praying, "Even so, come, Lord Jesus" (Rev 22:20, NASB).

On July 20, 1969, Neil Armstrong and Buzz Aldrin landed a lunar module called the Eagle on the moon. Incredibly, according to their flight plan, they were supposed to sleep before walking on the moon. Later Aldrin said that trying to sleep before walking on the moon "was like telling kids on Christmas morning they had to stay in bed until noon." Finally some officials in Houston gave them the go-ahead, and Armstrong took "one small step for man, one giant leap for mankind."

Some experiences are so great, you can hardly wait for them to happen. "The Lord himself will come down from heaven." First Thessalonians chapter 4 doesn't answer every question we have about the Lord's return, but it gives us several reasons to be ready and expectant, always hopeful, always watching and alert.

- *The Lord's return will be a time of earth-shattering noise.*

He will come "with a loud command, with the voice of the archangel and with the trumpet call of God" (v. 16). The Old Testament often mentions the sound of a trumpet in connection with times of celebration and triumph (for example, Isa 27:13; Joel 2:1; Zephaniah 1:14-16; see also 1 Cor 15:52).

- *The Lord's return will be a time of mind-blowing miracles.*

"And the dead in Christ will rise first" (v. 16). God already offered us a foretaste of this in the first century. When Jesus died on the cross,

"The tombs broke open and the bodies of many holy people who had died were raised to life. They came out of the tombs, and after Jesus' resurrection they went into the holy city and appeared to many people" (Matt 27:52,53). God has done great miracles in the past. But just wait till the dead are raised at the end of time. And not just one or two. God is going to raise up his people by the millions. As a country gospel song says, "Some glad morning when this life is o'er, I'll fly away."

> God is going to raise up his people by the millions.

- *The Lord's return will be a time of satisfying fellowship.*

"After that, we who are still alive and are left will be caught up with them in the clouds to meet the Lord in the air" (v. 17). This is going to be better than skydiving. It's going to be sky-rising! Christians who are alive at the time of Jesus' coming will be caught up in the clouds, lifted off the earth to join in the heavenly family reunion.

- *The Lord's return will initiate a time of everlasting worship.*

"And so we will be with the Lord forever" (v. 17). That's the main point. Our hope is not merely in a principle; it's in a Person. For a Christian, "to live is Christ, and to die is gain," and to die is to "depart and be with Christ" (Phil 1:21,23). Whatever Heaven is like, the main thing that will make it special is spending forever with Jesus.

Paul's point is that "those who have fallen asleep" or died will meet Jesus before those who are still alive at Jesus' coming. However, all of us will be together, equal in our relation to Jesus and "with the Lord forever" to offer him the worship he deserves (see Revelation 4–5).

Our Hope for the Future Keeps Us Going in the Present

"Therefore encourage each other with these words" (v. 18). What could be more encouraging than the assurance of eternal life with the Lord?

According to a newspaper account, a government agency sent a form letter to a South Carolina man who had died. The letter said, "Your food stamps will be stopped, effective in March, because we received notice that you passed away." Evidently a kindhearted government worker had tried to add a human touch by writing, "May God bless you." Then the form letter continued, "You may reapply if your circumstances change."

Thus far, the client has not reapplied.

But the day is going to come when our circumstances change. We're going to be raised from the dead. "Listen, I tell you a mystery:

We will not all sleep, but we will all be changed—in a flash, in the twinkling of an eye, at the last trumpet. For the trumpet will sound, the dead will be raised imperishable, and we will be changed" (1 Cor 15:51,52). We're going to be with the Lord forever.

> **The day is going to come when our circumstances change.**

When Candy and I were expecting our first child, I met a man who told me he felt sorry for us because we were going to have a baby. To him, the future looked so bleak he considered it a sad thing for a baby to be born.

Otis Palmer had a different point of view. Otis was a humble servant of God. He made several mission trips to Haiti, where he installed plumbing for Christian churches and schools and worked with children. When Otis learned he had terminal cancer, Candy and I, and two other friends, went to his house to visit him and his wife Anna Jean. We talked for a while, and then it became clear he was growing tired and we needed to go. I said, "Otis, we're going to pray. What would you like for us to pray about for you?"

This man was just a few days from death. He leaned back on his bed and thought for a long moment, and then he said, "Honestly, I can't think of a thing!" Then he said, "The Lord has been so good to me. He's given me everything I need and even more than I asked for." And his wife Anna Jean said, "He's at peace. We both are."

Otis lived and died with unquenchable hope in his heart. By the grace of God, so can we.

---

[1] Mark Jones, "The Lesson and Life," *The Lookout*, June 2, 2002, 12.
[2] Leon Morris, *The First and Second Epistles to the Thessalonians* (Grand Rapids: Eerdmans, 1959) 139.

86

✝

C
H
A
P
T
E
R

7 *Unquenchable Hope for the Future*

Developing Unquenchable Faith

1. Would you describe yourself as a hopeful person? Why, or why not?

2. What do you know for sure about the future return of Christ? What puzzles you about it?

3. What do you know for sure about life after death? What puzzles you about it?

4. How often do you think about your own death? About the death of a loved one? How does 1 Thessalonians 4:13-18 help you in times of grief? How might it help you face your own death with hope?

5. Together as a group, list some ways the reality of Christ's return affects your daily lives.

6. Do you know someone who is grieving the death of a loved one? What can your group do to encourage him or her in the coming week?

Memory Verse 1 Thess 4:16 *For the Lord himself will come down from heaven, with a loud command, with the voice of the archangel and with the trumpet call of God, and the dead in Christ will rise first.*

CHAPTER EIGHT

AN UNQUENCHABLE PASSION FOR CHANGING OUR CULTURE

1 THESSALONIANS 5:1-8

Ephesians 5:8 says, "For you were once darkness, but now you are light in the Lord. Live as children of light."

What does it mean to be "children of light" in a dark world? How does our faith relate to the world of sports, fashion, music, money, technology, and work? Should we embrace our culture, or withdraw from it? How can we reconcile the Bible verses that say, "Don't love the world" with the verses that say "Go into all the world" with the gospel?

How can we stand for life when abortion is considered legal and socially expedient? How can we stand for truth when popular philosophy says there are no moral absolutes? How can we stand for righteousness in an age when people with strong convictions are labeled as judgmental and intolerant? How can we love our neighbors when in most neighborhoods, people tend to stay to themselves? How can we point to Jesus as the unique Son of God and the only Savior in a culture that shrugs and says, "It doesn't matter what you believe, as long as you're sincere"? How can we teach our children that God comes first when most of the time our culture places God on the margin, instead of at the center, of what's going on?

How should Christians deal with our culture?

How should Christians deal with our culture? Believers have answered that question in different ways, and have tended to drift toward one of two extremes: *isolation* or *conformity*.

The *isolation* approach says:

- Remove yourself completely from the world. Pull away from your community, your schools, and your neighbors.
- Don't have any close friends who are non-Christians.
- Never read a secular book or magazine. Pay no attention to the news.
- Shun science and technology.
- Forget about art, music, movies, and the mall. Develop your own Christian subculture.

Isn't Jesus Lord over all of life?

But isn't Jesus Lord over all of life? Doesn't he call us to engage our culture and penetrate it with the good news? According to a recent survey, only 16 per cent of 18 to 22-year-olds have any contact at all with "organized religion." Yet their interest in spiritual things is even greater than in the past. Eighty-two per cent of them are asking questions about life after death. If Christians withdraw from their world, where will these young adults find the answers they're seeking? From Larry King? From movies and magazines? At the Barnes & Noble bookstore?[1]

At the other extreme, there's the *conformity* approach. It says:

- Just drift with the cultural tide, wherever it takes you. Uncritically adopt the mind-set of those around you.
- Don't concern yourself with what's modest and decent; dress however the fashion designers in Paris and New York tell you.
- If you see a movie, don't analyze and critique its message; absorb whatever Hollywood sends your way.
- At work or school, don't let others know you're a Christian; they might think you're weird.
- Don't encourage government officials to deal with issues of right and wrong or talk about their faith when discussing public policy; that violates the separation of church and state.
- In the church, don't step on anyone's toes. Get preachers to avoid the meat of God's Word and deliver painless, comfortable monologues.
- And evangelism? Forget it! Who are *you* to persuade others to change their points of view?

Conformity is for cowards, not for Christians.

But conformity is for cowards, not for Christians. Today, many Christians have let the culture squeeze them into its mold so that they have become indistinguishable from the world. Why should a seeker even go to church at all if what he finds there is exactly like the secular world with a little "God-talk" thrown in?

But there's a third alternative: *Jesus' approach*. Neither isolation nor conformity is the way of Christ. Jesus doesn't call us to isolate ourselves from the world, nor does he want us to conform to the world. He offers a different way of living—a third alternative. Christians aren't captive to our culture. Nor are we captives of the *counter*culture. Our allegiance is to the kingdom of God. Our citizenship is in Heaven.

How can we find the right balance? Radio host Dick Staub wrote a book called *Too Christian, Too Pagan*. He says if you really get serious about integrating your faith fully into your life in the world, you'll seem too Christian for your pagan friends and too pagan for your Christian friends![2]

Jesus had the perfect balance.

Jesus had the perfect balance. Sometimes he left the crowds and went off by himself to pray, but he was no isolationist. Other times, he went to dinner with well-known sinners. He rubbed shoulders with crowds in the marketplace, on the beach, by the roadside. He didn't deliver his most famous sermon from a church's pulpit, but on a mountainside. He was "in the world," but he was "not of the world."

The Pharisees didn't know what to do with Jesus, and most of them hated him because he didn't fit their mold. King Herod and Governor Pilate were fascinated with Jesus, and a bit afraid of him at the same time. He loved the people, but he told them hard truths—even if the crowds walked away because he didn't say or do what they expected. He offered forgiveness and grace, but he also called sinners to repentance and told them to "go and sin no more."

Jesus was impossible to pigeonhole. He didn't just march to the beat of a different drummer; he reinvented the drum.

Jesus didn't just march to the beat of a different drummer; he reinvented the drum.

He kept God's law, but he challenged commonly held traditions like what you were allowed to do on the Sabbath Day. Worshipers in Jerusalem had grown comfortable with the money changers in the temple, but Jesus threw them out. His disciples were drawn to him, but they couldn't quite figure him out. He fulfilled the Old Testament prophecies about the Messiah, but he didn't always act the way his countrymen expected the Messiah to act. Some tried to brand him a

An Unquenchable Passion for Changing Our Culture

rebel, yet they couldn't find him guilty of a single sin. Some said he was in cahoots with the devil, but everywhere Jesus went, he overthrew the devil's work.

Jesus told his disciples to be shrewd as serpents and harmless as doves (Matt 10:16). Be sharp, but be pure. Be involved, but be different. Communicate, but keep your distinctiveness. Connect, but don't conform. Be "in the world, but not of the world." Don't let your culture shape you; you shape *it*! Be an influencer—a force for godliness.

> **Connect, but don't conform.**

If you have an unquenchable passion to change your culture for the better, 1 Thessalonians 5:1-8 has some important lessons for you to consider.

Do Not Be Sidetracked by Pointless Speculation

"Now, brothers, about times and dates we do not need to write to you" (v. 1). Some Christians have brought dishonor upon the church by engaging in date-setting and wild predictions about the Lord's return. In 1978 a Texas preacher made headlines by predicting that the Lord would return on April 1, 1980. The day came and went and nothing happened, and a lot of people chuckled about the appropriateness of the date—April Fools' Day. Paul warns us not to get involved in pointless speculation. We dishonor our Lord and we look foolish to the world when we proclaim an inaccurate message supposedly from God. (See Jer 23:16-32.)

"For you know very well that the day of the Lord will come like a thief in the night" (v. 2). Christ will return at a time when many do not expect him, so we should be ready for his return at all times (Mark 13:32-37). It's too late to prepare for a test when the professor puts the test paper on your desk. It's too late to prepare for a storm when the wind is already gusting. Someday it will be too late to prepare for the coming of the Lord (Matt 24:42-51). "While people are saying, 'Peace and safety,' destruction will come on them suddenly, as labor pains on a pregnant woman, and they will not escape" (v. 3).

Be Alert and Self-Controlled

The day of the Lord, however, need not overtake God's people with complete surprise, for we should be watching for it at all times. "But you, brothers, are not in darkness so that this day should surprise you like a thief" (v. 4).

God Wants Us to Walk in the Light, Not in the Darkness.

"You are all sons of the light and sons of the day. We do not belong to the night or to the darkness" (v. 5).

Most of the time we take light for granted. The sun comes up each morning. We flip on the light switch in our homes. If you want a midnight snack, there's even a little light in the refrigerator.

Imagine what it would be like to live in total darkness. The Bible says "God is light; in him is no darkness at all" (1 John 1:5). When God created the heavens and the earth, he said, "Let there be light." God's Word is a lamp to our feet and a light to our path (Ps 119:105). Jesus said, "I am the light of the world. Whoever follows me will never walk in darkness, but will have the light of life" (John 8:12).

Paul says we are "sons of the light." There are several qualities of light that help us appreciate what this means.

While light stays essentially the same, we can find new ways to shine it. In Bible times, a homeowner would use a candle, a torch, or an oil lamp (a bowl of olive oil with a cloth wick floating in it). Two centuries ago gas lamps were developed. One century ago, Thomas Edison invented the electric light bulb. Then along came battery-powered flashlights, and eventually lava lamps and strobe lights. Today we can use laser beams for surgery. We keep finding new ways to let light shine, but light itself remains basically the same. Likewise, God's truth always remains the same, but each generation needs to figure out some fresh new ways to shine it.

> We keep finding new ways to let light shine,
> but light itself remains basically the same.

There's something mysterious about light. Scientists still don't know all there is to know about light. Is it a wave? Is it a particle? How does it move with lightning speed, yet most of the time we're not even aware it's moving at all? There's something mysterious about faith, too. I can't always explain how God answers prayer, but I know he does. I can't fully explain Heaven, but I am confident it's real.

Light works quietly. You never *hear* light. It never makes a sound. It doesn't attract attention to itself—it just helps you see other things more clearly. If you're lighting your world, you don't call attention to yourself, but to the Lord (see Matt 5:16).

Light shouldn't be hidden. In Matthew 5:14 Jesus said, "You are the light of the world; a city on a hill cannot be hidden." In that famous verse, he used the plural form of the word "you." He was not only talking about one person individually; he was talking about his people collectively. Did

An Unquenchable Passion for Changing Our Culture

you ever drive through the countryside on a dark night? Far off in the distance you can see the glow of city lights ahead of you. I grew up on a farm 50 miles from Cincinnati, but on a clear summer night you could see the glow of the city from our front yard. You wouldn't notice one little light shining by itself, but when lots of lights combine together, you can't miss the glow. That's how it is in the church.

Jesus said, "Neither do people light a lamp and put it under a bowl. Instead they put it on its stand, and it gives light to everyone in the house" (Matt 5:15). There were no matches in Jesus' day. To start a fire, you had to use pieces of flint or rub two sticks together like Boy Scouts do. It wasn't easy to get a fire going, so once you did, you wouldn't light a lamp and then put it under a bowl where it would quickly go out. You'd put it on a stand where it would give light to everyone. Are we reflecting the light of Jesus in our neighborhoods, at work, at school, and in all our relationships with people around us?

God Wants Us to Be Alert, Not Sleepy.

"So then, let us not be like others, who are asleep, but let us be alert and self-controlled" (v. 6).

Too many Christians have "Eutychus syndrome." Remember Eutychus? He's the fellow who fell asleep during the apostle Paul's sermon. As the sermon went long, Eutychus's eyelids began drooping, his head started bobbing, the lamps were flickering in his eyes, and he fell asleep (literally!). He fell out of a window three stories from the ground, and he "was picked up dead." But Paul wrapped his arms around Eutychus, and God restored him to life. They went back upstairs, had something to eat, and then (since I am a preacher, this part makes me chuckle) Paul went on and finished his sermon, talking until daylight! (See Acts 20:7-12.)

> The Eutychus syndrome is all too common among Christians. We are spiritual sleepwalkers.

The Eutychus syndrome is all too common among Christians. We are spiritual sleepwalkers. We eat too much, spend too much time with video games, get hooked on soap operas, invest inordinate amounts of energy and money on sports, and allow worldly things to steal our alertness. Jesus' message to today's sleepwalking saints is the same thing he told the first-century church in Sardis: "Wake up! Strengthen what remains and is about to die, for I have not found your deeds complete in the sight of my God. Remember, therefore, what you have received and heard; obey it, and repent. But if you do not wake up, I

93

‡

C
H
A
P
T
E
R

8

An Unquenchable Passion for Changing Our Culture

will come like a thief, and you will not know at what time I will come to you" (Rev 3:2,3).

God Wants Us to Be Self-Controlled, Not Drunk.

"For those who sleep, sleep at night, and those who get drunk, get drunk at night" (v. 7).

One way Christians demonstrate self-control is by avoiding destructive and addictive behaviors like drunkenness. Alcohol abuse clouds judgment, wrecks marriages and families, wastes money, takes lives on the highway, lessens productivity at work, causes illness and disease, sets a bad example for young people, and makes its users do foolish things they later regret.

When my daughter Melinda left home to attend a university, her Uncle Jim (my older brother who is a longtime high school teacher) wrote her a letter encouraging her to be faithful to the Lord on the university campus. In his letter he wrote:

> I found out very quickly in college that most kids are looking for leadership and guidance from their classmates and friends.
>
> When I began as a freshman at Ohio State I was very worried about drinking. I had been told that everyone drank in college on weekends and I knew I didn't want to do it. How could I survive if I was the only one who didn't drink?
>
> The very first Friday evening we were in school some upperclassmen came into our dorm and invited several of us freshmen to go drinking with them. I was really scared. Everyone stood around and looked at each other so I spoke up and said I didn't like to drink and I would prefer to go to a movie and get soft drinks. Immediately several others spoke up and said they wanted to go with me. It was amazing! From that day forward the issue of drinking was never a problem and I'm convinced that others were happy I simply spoke up and said what I knew to be right. Even the ones who drank often said to me that they wished they could say no to drinking.
>
> We often think we are the only ones who want to do the right thing, when in reality others are waiting for a leader. I urge you to be a leader. You will be surprised at your influence.

> ### THE SALT OF THE EARTH
>
> What did the Lord mean when he said, "You are the salt of the earth" (Matthew 5:13)?
>
> Salt was valuable in Bible times. Most people ate a simple diet, and salt added flavor to meat or bread made from wheat or barley.

John the Baptist ate locusts, which surely tasted better with a little salt! Roman soldiers were paid a regular salt ration, which in Latin was called a *salarium*. (This is where we get our word "salary" and the expression that a man is "worth his salt.")

Salt's white, clean-looking crystals served as symbols of purity and sacrifice. According to Leviticus 2:13, the priests added salt to all the grain offerings presented on the altar. Salt also brings to mind God's judgment, for the first time salt is mentioned in the Bible is when Lot's wife disobeyed God by looking back at the cities of Sodom and Gomorrah, and she became a pillar of salt (Gen 19:26).

In biblical times, salt mainly was used as a preservative. There were no refrigerators or freezers in Jesus' day. If you butchered a steer or a sheep, the only way to keep the meat from spoiling was to dry it and cure it with salt. Jesus lived in Galilee, where one of the most popular foods was a small salted fish similar to a sardine. (Two of these small fish were probably the kind Jesus used when he fed the 5,000.)

The Christian life is anything but bland, dull, and tasteless. There should be a different flavor to our lives because we love the Lord. There should be a holy zest, a salty tang to our lives. When we're around someone with a rotten attitude, we need to be salt. Sin spoils things; God's people need to preserve what is good.

Salt also makes people thirsty. We need to talk and act in a way that makes others thirsty for God. Colossians 4:6 says, "Let your conversation be always full of grace, seasoned with salt, so that you may know how to answer everyone." When I was about 14 years old, some young men—students at Kentucky Christian College—stayed at our house for the weekend. They talked about football and music and girls, and we laughed a lot. But these young men also were very serious about the Lord. They were more fun than most Christians I knew, yet they were also more serious about God than most people I knew. Like "salt," those guys made me thirsty. They made me want a faith filled with humor, joy, adventure, and purpose.

If you want your life to make a difference, don't lose your "saltiness."

God Wants Us to Be Protected, Not Defenseless.

"But since we belong to the day, let us be self-controlled, putting on faith and love as a breastplate, and the hope of salvation as a helmet" (v. 8). Paul uses a similar analogy in Ephesians chapter 6, where he says we must "be strong in the Lord and in his mighty power," and put on the "whole armor of God" so we can take our stand against the devil's schemes.

An Unquenchable Passion for Changing Our Culture 8

If you're a soldier, you don't just wander into battle wearing sneakers and a T-shirt; you put on your armor. During the war in Iraq, American soldiers were well equipped with state-of-the-art weapons, bulletproof helmets and vests, gas masks, and antidotes for chemical weapons. They were still in great danger, but think where they'd have been without their equipment.

There's a spiritual battle going on, and we need God's protection in the fight. The main battlefields of our culture wars are not in church buildings but on the turf of daily life. We don't wage war as the world does, but God provides us with spiritual weapons like the Word of God and prayer that are more effective than anything the world offers. (See 2 Cor 10:3-5 and Prov 21:22.)

> There's a spiritual battle going on,
> and we need God's protection in the fight.

Christians do not have to use the world's weapons in the spiritual battles we fight. We oppose abortion, but we don't resort to name-calling and violence or bomb abortion clinics; we support crisis pregnancy centers and adoptive parents who offer hope and positive solutions. We are concerned about crime and injustice, but we don't have to go into the woods and form a Christian militia; we support prison ministries that reach out to prisoners and their families. We get involved in urban ministries that serve families, help kids succeed in school, and help to prevent crime before it happens. We don't just give speeches about poverty and homelessness; we support Christ-centered groups that address these problems in positive and practical ways.

> Christians do not have to use the
> world's weapons in the spiritual battles we fight.

Jesus didn't pray that his people would be removed from our culture, but he prayed that in the midst of it we will be protected from Satan. He said, "My prayer is not that you take them out of the world but that you protect them from the evil one. They are not of the world, even as I am not of it. Sanctify them by the truth; your word is truth. As you sent me into the world, I have sent them into the world" (John 17:15-18). A Christian's relationship to the world is like a boat. It's good for a boat to be in the water, but it's bad if there's too much water in the boat. Christians need to be in the world. Jesus sends us there. But we need to be careful not to get too much of the world into us.

We don't have to fight this battle alone. Jesus prayed, "May they be

An Unquenchable Passion for Changing Our Culture

brought to complete unity to let the world know that you sent me" (John 17:23). Division in the church dims our light and weakens our influence. We need each other. Christian unity is one of our most powerful spiritual weapons. If we're going to win this cultural battle, it won't be because of our own strength but because of the power God provides through his Holy Spirit working in the church.

> **Christian unity is one of our most powerful spiritual weapons.**

Practical Steps for Culture-Changers

Here are four practical steps we can take as Christians if we want to make a difference in our culture for the sake of the Lord.

1. *Before you try to change your world, ask God to change you.* In a Peanuts cartoon, Charlie Brown says, "I would like to change the world." Lucy says, "I would start with you." It's good to start with ourselves.

Is your own heart right before God? Has your salt lost its saltiness? Have you been hiding your light under a basket?

2. *Don't run from people; relate to them.* Jesus was a friend of sinners. Don't belittle them; befriend them. Non-Christians aren't arguments to be won, they're souls to be loved. If you build relationships of honesty and trust, God will turn those relationships into bridges for the love of Christ to cross.

3. *Don't conform; be transformed.* We need to discipline our minds to think Christianly. Analyze the world from a biblical perspective. Whether it's a song on the radio, a news story on the Internet, or a story line on a TV show, evaluate its message and filter out the ideas that displease God. The Bible says, "Do not conform any longer to the pattern of this world, but be transformed by the renewing of your mind" (Rom 12:2). Don't just mindlessly soak up the culture around you. Let God shape your worldview.

4. *Don't isolate; penetrate.* Ministry doesn't just happen in a church building. Be an involved and informed Christian citizen. Vote in elections. Voice your opinions about moral issues affecting your nation. Take your faith with you as you get involved in school activities, sports leagues, and community events. Be a good neighbor.

Paul was flexible with his methods but firm in his message. He never compromised God's truth and never wavered about his convictions, but he related to people in a way they could understand. He said, "I have become all things to all men so that by all possible means I might save some" (1 Cor 9:22).

An Unquenchable Passion for Changing Our Culture

A woman who had never attended our church before came to a Bible class one evening. After the class was over, I asked how she happened to come to the church. She mentioned the name of a man who works at her company who's a member of the church. She said, "I've watched him at work, and there's something different and special about him." She said, "Whatever he has, I want that in my life." That man is being salt and light at his job.

Daniel and Nehemiah were salt and light in the government, where they served as right-hand men to kings. The apostle Peter was salt and light when he preached the gospel before the Jewish Supreme Court. The apostle Paul was salt and light when he testified about Christ before the leading thinkers in Athens. The Lord wants Christians to salt the earth and light the world in factories and auto repair shops, in school classrooms and corporate boardrooms. We need Christian doctors and nurses, cooks and coaches, lawyers and merchants, bankers, musicians, athletes, artists, salespeople, professors, and janitors.

We are children of light. Let's make a difference in our world.

---

[1] See Dick Staub, *Too Christian, Too Pagan* (Grand Rapids: Zondervan, 2000) 15, 16.
[2] Ibid., 16.

Developing Unquenchable Faith

1. What do you think it means to be "children of light" instead of walking in darkness?

2. The author of this book makes the point that Christians often tend to adopt one of two extremes in regard to their surrounding culture: isolation or conformity. Do you agree with this analysis? Why, or why not? Can you think of examples of both extremes?

3. *"Be involved, but be different. Communicate, but keep your distinctiveness. Connect, but don't conform. Be 'in the world, but not of the world.' Don't let your culture shape you; you shape it! Be an influencer—a force for godliness."* Do you think it's really possible to do this? If so, does this statement describe the way you live your life most of the time? Why, or why not?

4. What bothers you about some of the trends you observe in our culture? As a group, make a list of some characteristics of "darkness" rather than "light" you observe in today's world. After you make your list, discuss what Christians could do to address and change some of these problem areas.

5. Close the group session by praying for:
   - The light of Christ to be evident in your community;
   - Boldness and wisdom to be a light for Christ in your own home, school, or workplace this week.

Memory Verse
1 Thess 5:5-6

You are all sons of the light and sons of the day. We do not belong to the night or to the darkness. So then, let us not be like others, who are asleep, but let us be alert and self-controlled.

CHAPTER NINE

UNQUENCHABLE ENCOURAGEMENT

1 THESSALONIANS 5:9-28

I was driving along a city street when I noticed a sign in front of a church that evidently was announcing the title of the minister's upcoming sermon. The sign said simply, "Discouragement: Sunday, 10:00 a.m." That's not a smart way for a church to advertise!

How many discouraging things happened to you last week? Just driving to work can be aggravating. There's a rule I've learned to apply on the highway: "The shortest distance between two points . . . is usually under construction."

Discouragement can come from something as serious as the death of a loved one, or as trivial as your favorite team losing a game they should have won. It can come from a problem as far-reaching as war in the Middle East, or as personal as your own battle with anger, an eating disorder, or low self-esteem.

A demolition crew tore down Cincinnati's old baseball stadium, Cinergy Field, with a series of blasts that imploded the stadium in just 37 seconds. Meanwhile, it took a construction crew more than three years to build Cincinnati's new Great American Ballpark. It's easy to tear things down, but it takes time and effort to build them up.

> It's easy to tear things down,
> but it takes time and effort to build them up.

First Thessalonians 5:11 says, "Therefore encourage one another and build each other up, just as in fact you are doing." In a world that tears people down, we are God's construction crew. The Scripture says, "We love because he first loved us" (1 John 4:19). It's the same way with encouragement.

We Encourage Others, Because God First Encouraged Us

"For God did not appoint us to suffer wrath but to receive salvation through our Lord Jesus Christ. He died for us so that, whether we are awake or asleep, we may live together with him" (vv. 9,10). The most encouraging news we will ever hear is the fact that God loves us. Whether we're awake or asleep, healthy or sick, rich or poor, happy or sad, we aren't alone. We "live together with him."

> **The most encouraging news we will ever hear is the fact that God loves us.**

The Bible tells about a time in the life of King David when a group of enemy raiders burned a town called Ziklag to the ground and captured the wives, sons, and daughters of David and his men. The Bible says, "David and his men wept aloud until they had no strength left to weep" (1 Samuel 30:4).

David's men held him responsible because they were away from home fighting under his leadership while their families were attacked. They became so bitter and angry, they talked about stoning David to death.

But then the Bible says, "David encouraged himself in the Lord his God" (1 Sam 30:6, KJV). Eventually David and his men got their wives and children back, along with all of the things the enemy raiders had taken. Sometimes there's no one else to encourage us except the Lord our God—but in those times, we discover that God is enough.

We can encourage others because of what God has done for us.

Who Needs Our Encouragement?

In the verses that follow in First Thessalonians 5, the apostle Paul mentions several groups of people who need us to build them up.

Leaders Need Our Encouragement.

"Now we ask you, brothers, to respect those who work hard among you, who are over you in the Lord and who admonish you. Hold them in the highest regard in love because of their work" (vv. 12,13).

Leaders aren't perfect, but healthy leadership is God-ordained and it's for our own good.

Unquenchable Encouragement 9

- A child needs to respect her parents.
- Church members need to respect the church's elders.
- An employee needs to respect her boss.
- A student needs to respect his teacher.
- A citizen needs to respect the government authorities.

> **Leaders aren't perfect, but healthy leadership is God-ordained and it's for our own good.**

The word translated "respect" in verse 12 literally means to "know" our leaders. It's easy to criticize our leaders if we see them as distant figures, aloof and unapproachable. But when you get to know them and you see their love for the Lord, you're more likely to trust them and give them the benefit of the doubt.

Paul says to respect "those who work hard among you." Church leadership is hard work. Leaders carry heavy burdens. If you've never been an elder in a church, or served in some other position of leadership, you may have no idea about the long hours leaders spend shepherding and advising people, visiting the sick, counseling those in crisis, laboring in prayer, and making difficult decisions. Stuart Briscoe once said that a minister needs "the mind of a scholar, the heart of a child, and the hide of a rhinoceros."

Michael Deaver served as Deputy Chief of Staff during the Reagan administration. On the morning of President Reagan's first inauguration, Deaver was concerned because it appeared his boss had overslept. He knocked on the president's bedroom door and said, "Sir, it's 8:30 in the morning. In about two hours, you're going to become the 40th president of the United States!"

Reagan sleepily poked his head out from under the covers and joked, "Do I *have* to?" Most leaders feel that way sometimes.

Hebrews 13:17 says, "Obey your leaders and submit to their authority. They watch over you as men who must give an account. Obey them so that their work will be a joy, not a burden, for that would be of no advantage to you."

Leaders have a tough job. Don't be a thorn in their side. Make their work a joy. Don't be a burden; be a blessing. Nobody wins when leaders and followers are at odds with each other. This doesn't mean we never speak up, disagree, or express our own opinions about things, but it does mean we should be encouraging and cooperative toward our leaders.

> **Nobody wins when leaders and followers are at odds with each other.**

"Hold them in the highest regard in love because of their work." Don't put them on a pedestal, but honor them. Love them. Encourage them. And as verse 13 says, "Live in peace with each other," for leaders grow weary of dealing with conflicts and quarrels. Our leaders need encouragement.

Uninvolved People Need Our Encouragement.

"And we urge you, brothers, warn those who are idle" (v. 14). The word translated "idle" is a military term that referred to a soldier who was out of step or loafing while he should have been on duty. The King James Version translates it "unruly." It describes someone who is not playing by the rules, not carrying his share of the load.

Proverbs 18:9 says, "One who is slack in his work is brother to one who destroys." If you're not helping the Lord's work move forward, you're holding it back. If you're not doing your part, someone else has to work harder.

In the church, everyone doesn't need to do the same thing. But everyone needs to do *something* to advance the cause of Christ. Get involved. Find a place to serve. And encourage others to get involved too.

Timid People Need Our Encouragement.

Verse 14 says, "Encourage the timid." Instead of "timid," other translations of the Bible say "faint-hearted" or "feeble-minded." The word literally means "small souled." Encourage "those whose souls are small." These are the people who lack confidence—the shy, the fearful, the timid.

> One of the greatest gifts you can give is to befriend and encourage those who lack confidence and help them reach their full potential.

This is a much larger group of people than you might think. One of the greatest gifts you can give is to befriend and encourage those who lack confidence and help them reach their full potential. What about the shy kid in the high school group, the timid little girl who lives next door, or the quiet senior adult?

Weak People Need Our Encouragement.

Verse 14 says, "Help the weak." Right now some members of your church are probably experiencing financial weakness; they are out of work or facing a mountain of debt. Others are experiencing physical weakness; they are hospitalized, facing surgery or a prolonged illness. Some must deal with emotional weakness.

- After years of marriage, a man's wife dies, and every time he sits in church by himself, his eyes fill with tears.
- The church gives flowers to the ladies on Mother's Day, and a young woman privately grieves because she had an abortion five years ago.
- On Father's Day, a young man feels angry because his dad was never there for him.
- A middle-aged couple grieve because their son or daughter has strayed from God and broken their hearts.
- A successful-looking businessman fights a daily battle with depression.

Still others deal with spiritual weakness. Jude verse 22 says, "Be merciful to those who doubt." Most of us have times when our faith comes under attack, when we wonder if God is really there, when it seems like our prayers go unanswered, when our spiritual energy feels depleted. In times of weakness, we need to encourage one another.

The bottom line? *Everyone needs our encouragement.* "Be patient with everyone. Make sure that nobody pays back wrong for wrong, but always try to be kind to each other and to everyone else" (vv. 14,15).

> **The bottom line is that everyone needs our encouragement.**

Before the evangelist Billy Sunday went to preach in a city, it was his custom to ask city leaders for a list of people in the city who needed prayer so he could pray for them in advance of the meeting. When Sunday went to Columbus, Ohio, he wrote to the mayor and asked him for a list of people in Columbus who needed prayer. The mayor sent him back a copy of the Columbus phone book! Everybody in the city needed prayer, he said.

How Can We Give Encouragement?

There are several practical ways we can offer encouragement to others.

✝ We Can Encourage through Spoken Words.

Proverbs 18:21 says, "The tongue has the power of life and death." Do you use your tongue to encourage? Ella Wilcox wrote, "A pat on the back is only a few vertebrae removed from a kick in the pants, but it is miles ahead in results." Someone has said there are two kinds of people in our lives: balcony people—the great encouragers who cheer us on and lift our vision, and basement people—the folks who are never satisfied, who drag us down.

Some people are like spurs and others are like spears. "Spurs" are the helpful ones who prod you on to "love and good deeds" (Heb 10:24). "Spears" are the hurtful folks whose words stab and wound. Some people make you want to "brace" yourself when you encounter them because their words are usually negative and critical. Others make you want to "embrace" them because they are warm, loving, and a joy to be around.

> Some people are like spurs and others are like spears.

We Can Encourage through Written Words.

The apostle Paul filled his letters to the churches with words of encouragement. We can do this too by writing notes of appreciation for others.

I have a minister friend who spends the last 15 minutes of every workday writing notes of appreciation before he goes home in the evening. This habit not only encourages the people who receive his letters; it also helps him end his workday with a positive attitude about the people in his church.

A Daily Dose of Vitamin E

Everyone needs a daily dose of Vitamin E (Encouragement). Hebrews 3:13 says, "But encourage one another daily, as long as it is called Today, so that none of you may be hardened by sin's deceitfulness." This verse shows us several important facts about encouragement.

(1) Encouragement requires PERSONAL INTERACTION. "Encourage *one another.*" You can only get so much encouragement from reading a book, listening to a radio preacher, or taking a walk outdoors. The greatest encouragement comes from "one another-ing" in the church.

(2) Encouragement is a PERISHABLE COMMODITY. "Encourage one another *daily.*" The reservoir of encouragement needs to be refilled every 24 hours. Encouragement is like manna from above— daily bread for the soul.

(3) Encouragement is PREVENTIVE MEDICINE. *"So that none of you may be hardened by sin's deceitfulness."* We are less likely to fall into sin if we have someone encouraging us to do the right thing.

We Can Encourage by Maintaining a Positive Attitude.

In a burst of short, staccato phrases, 1 Thessalonians 5:16-22 lists seven attitudes that turn those who possess them into effective encouragers:

1. JOY. "Be joyful always" (v. 16). This doesn't mean plastering on a fake smile. All of us have problems and feel down now and then. But if you're going to be an encourager, you can't be a whiner, always negative, always complaining and pointing out the worst. When the joy of Christ is in your heart, you can always demonstrate a steady cheerfulness, a positive attitude, and a strong faith.

2. PRAYER. "Pray continually" (v. 17). The King James Version translates, "Pray without ceasing." That sounds like a hard command, doesn't it? Perhaps we should see it not only as a command but also as a promise. It's our privilege to live constantly in the presence of God. If someone said, "Breathe without ceasing," you wouldn't consider it a burden. You need oxygen to live. Breathing is a natural response. If someone said, "Let your heart beat continually," you wouldn't think it unreasonable. It's what your body must do to survive. "Pray without ceasing" is a natural thing for a Christian to do. God is always ready to engage in conversation with us. Even a great leader like the apostle Paul recognized his need for prayer. He urged the Thessalonians, "Brothers, pray for us" (v. 25).

3. THANKSGIVING. "Give thanks in all circumstances, for this is God's will for you in Christ Jesus" (v. 18). Ingratitude rots the soul. The Israelites enjoyed the Promised Land's good food and refreshing freedoms, but drifted into self-sufficiency and ingratitude (Deut 8:6-20; 2 Chronicles 26:15,16). When Jesus healed ten men of leprosy, 90 per cent of them gave him no thanks (Luke 17:11-19). If we have experienced God's kindness, only the callousness of sin could make us ungrateful (Rom 1:21).

4. ZEAL. "Do not put out the Spirit's fire" (v. 19). The King James Version says, "Quench not the Spirit." This has been one of the themes we've traced all the way through First Thessalonians. God wants us to have unquenchable faith.

There are two ways to put out a fire. You can smother it (as a fire extinguisher does) or you can simply let it burn out of fuel. The fire of God's Spirit cools if you let your own doubts or faithless people throw a wet blanket on your faith. And the fire cools when you don't feed on God's Word, share your faith with others, participate in Christian worship and fellowship, and do whatever else fuels the fire.

This verse makes me want to be filled with unquenchable zeal for my Lord. I want to be able to say:

> You can't put the fire out.
> You can throw cold water on my emotions,
> But there will still be a flame burning deep in my soul.
> You can push my body to the limit, but the fire of His Word
> Will still burn in my bones.
> You can mock my faith and tell me the Bible isn't true,
> But you can't put the fire out.
>
> I might bend, but I won't break.
> I might feel dejected, but I won't be defeated.
> I might be down, but I'm not out.
> I may feel weary, but I don't have to worry.
> I may be tired, but I'm not terrified—
> Because you can't put the fire out.
>
> I have sinned, but Jesus loves me still.
> I have failed, but Jesus never will.
> When I'm broke, I'm not broken.
> When I'm sick, I'm not stuck.
> When I'm poor, He keeps on giving.
> When I die, I'll keep on living—
> Because His Spirit burns within me,
> And you can't put the fire out!

5. TEACHABLE SPIRIT. "Do not treat prophecies with contempt" (v. 20). In the first century, this meant listening carefully to inspired speakers whose messages came directly from God. In our day, it means listening carefully to the teaching and preaching of God's written Word, the Bible. The apostle Paul considered public reading of Scripture so important, he solemnly instructed the Thessalonians, "I charge you before the Lord to have this letter read to all the brothers" (v. 27). If we're going to encourage others, we should have a humble, teachable spirit.

6. DISCERNING MIND. "Test everything. Hold on to the good" (v. 21). While we should be teachable, we shouldn't be gullible. The Lord doesn't want us to believe everything we see on TV, read in a book, or hear in the classroom. Deceptive people and ideas may look good on the surface, but they're dangerous and can lead our minds away from our "sincere and pure devotion to Christ" (2 Cor 11:3).

7. RESISTANCE TO SIN. "Avoid every kind of evil" (v. 22). The King James Version says, "Abstain from all appearance of evil." Don't flirt with it; flee from it.

We Can Encourage through Appropriate Physical Touch.

"Greet all the brothers with a holy kiss" (v. 26). In some cultures it's still customary to greet each other with a kiss on the cheek. In other cultures, people show respect by bowing to one another. Some of us are more comfortable expressing our greetings through hugs, handshakes, or a friendly hand on the shoulder. However you do it, never underestimate the value of appropriate touch. For some who attend your church week after week, the only meaningful physical contact they receive all week may be the handshake they receive at the church door on Sunday morning. And notice that Paul says to greet "*all* the brothers"—not just the ones who look beautiful, or those who are the most fun to be around.

Cam Huxford tells about a time when he was in a near-fatal car accident while a student in Bible college years ago. His mom, a single parent, came to Atlanta to stay with him while he recovered. Cam says, "Her husband was in Heaven, her church family hours away, her son seriously injured. It was a hard, lonely time for her. Ross Dampier, a local preacher, came to my room and prayed for us. As he did, he put his hand on my mother's back, and she just sobbed. To this day, she remembers the comfort she received from that simple touch."[1]

The Unquenchable Encouragement of God

The greatest encourager of all is the Lord God himself. As he prepares to conclude his first letter to the Thessalonians, Paul prays a special prayer of blessing for his readers: "May God himself, the God of peace, sanctify you through and through. May your whole spirit, soul and body be kept blameless at the coming of our Lord Jesus Christ. The one who calls you is faithful and he will do it" (vv. 23,24).

Notice what these verses tell us about God:
- He is the God of peace.
- He is the God of holiness, who desires to "sanctify" us (set us apart as holy) in every way.
- He is faithful.
- He will do what he promises to do.

And notice what these verses tell us about ourselves:
- God cares about every part of our being (spirit, soul, body).
- God wants us to be "blameless" when Jesus comes again.

How can we be blameless before God? Only by God's grace—his unmerited favor and forgiveness. Thankfully, his grace is abundant and free, so Paul ends this letter with another prayer of blessing: "The grace of our Lord Jesus Christ be with you" (v. 28).

The Lord's amazing grace is with us. In a very discouraging world, that's a reason to be unquenchably encouraged!

---

[1] Cam Huxford, "Encouraged to Encourage!" *The Lookout*, June 24, 2001.

Developing Unquenchable Faith

1. What (or who) has discouraged you in recent days? What (or who) has encouraged you?

2. List some people in the following categories who could use some encouragement from you or your group:
   - Those in positions of leadership
   - Those who are "idle" or uninvolved in the church
   - Those who are timid
   - Those who are currently experiencing some sort of weakness (physically, financially, emotionally, or spiritually).

3. As a group, pray for the people you listed above; then prepare and send an encouraging note or a card to each of the people for whom you prayed.

4. Would others describe you as a person who has a positive attitude most of the time? Why, or why not?

5. Read aloud the short list of commands recorded in 1 Thessalonians 5:16-22. Which of these commands is easiest for you to obey? Which is the hardest? Explain.

6. Close your group by reading the prayer of blessing recorded in 1 Thessalonians 5:23,24.

Memory Verse 1 Thess 5:11

Therefore encourage one another and build each other up, just as in fact you are doing.

CHAPTER TEN

AN UNQUENCHABLE DETERMINATION TO PERSEVERE

2 THESSALONIANS 1:1-12

One letter to the Thessalonians wasn't enough. A second letter was needed to further encourage the church and to correct some misguided excitement the first letter generated about the return of Christ.

Like the first epistle, 2 Thessalonians comes from the inspired pen of the apostle Paul, along with his colleagues Silas and Timothy. Both letters are addressed "to the church of the Thessalonians in God our Father and the Lord Jesus Christ." Both begin with a greeting that blesses the readers with God's "grace and peace" (1 Thess 1:1,2; 2 Thess 1:1,2).

Spiritual Staying Power

Paul continues the encouraging tone found in his first epistle by commending the Thessalonians for the way they continued to grow in faith and in love. "We ought always to thank God for you, brothers, and rightly so, because your faith is growing more and more, and the love every one of you has for each other is increasing" (v. 3).

It was especially important for these first-century Christians to keep growing in faith and love because they were facing many hardships. Paul continues, "Therefore, among God's churches we boast about your perseverance and faith in all the persecutions and trials you are enduring" (v. 4). In spite of everything that was working against them, the Thessalonians had an unquenchable determination to persevere.

Perseverance is spiritual staying power. According to Gary Weedman, the Thessalonians' "endurance is not a passive resignation, but rather a stalwart and active confidence in the face of oppression."[1] As someone has said, "Christians are like tea bags; you won't know what's inside of them until you throw them into some hot water."

What kind of persecution did the Thessalonians face? It's likely they endured personal insults like the kind described in 1 Peter 2:12; 3:16; and 4:4. Other first-century believers suffered mistreatment of various kinds including imprisonment, confiscation of property, and even death (Heb 10:32-34; Acts 7:54-60). Jesus pronounced a special blessing on those who are persecuted for righteousness' sake (Matt 5:11,12)—a beatitude with special significance for Christians like those in the Thessalonian church. From the very beginning when their church was first planted in Thessalonica, the believers there had been misunderstood and falsely accused (Acts 17:5-9), yet they persevered in their faith.

Professor Leon Morris comments that our "faith is not some fragile thing, to be kept in a kind of spiritual cotton wool, insulated from all shocks. It is robust. It is to be manifested in the fires of trouble, and in the furnace of affliction. . . . The very troubles and afflictions which the world heaps on the believer become, under God, the means of making him what he ought to be."[2] Strange as it sounds, an easier, more comfortable life may actually make it harder to grow in our faith.

The Bible says that the testing of faith "develops perseverance," and "perseverance must finish its work so that you may be mature and complete, not lacking anything" (James 1:3,4).

How Mature Are You?

Hebrews 6:1 says we should "go on to maturity." That's one of the purposes of the church—to help everyone grow spiritually, emotionally, mentally—in every way, until we grow up and become fully-developed followers of Christ (Eph 4:13).

Let's be honest. A lot of our problems are caused by our own immaturity. The number one reason couples struggle in marriage is just that they need to grow up. Many church problems arise because we're childish and self-centered. We get into trouble in our relationships with others because of our immature words, decisions, and actions.

Maturity isn't the same as age. You can be a Christian for 50 years, and still be immature. Maturity isn't the same as appearance, and it isn't just a matter of achievement. You can accomplish a lot and still be immature. Maturity isn't just a matter of academics. There's even

---

a degree called "Master of Divinity," but no one has totally mastered the study of God!

Maturity means being complete—fully developed—the person God made you to be. Jesus Christ is the perfect picture of maturity. God can even use our suffering to help us become more like him (Rom 5:3-5).

There's a part of us that would like to glide through life without any problems or bumps in the road, but God's Word is honest. Hardship is par for the course. We should expect to face trials of "many kinds" (Jas 1:2).

What makes it difficult for you to persevere in your faith? What about all those little daily irritations you have to endure? Traffic wears on your nerves as you commute to work. Your kids do chin-ups in the bathroom and yank the towel rack off the wall. A rock falls off the dump-truck ahead of your car and cracks your windshield. You stand in a long line at the grocery store waiting to pay for your groceries, but the person ahead of you is paying with a credit card, and the machine malfunctions so you have to wait while they repair it (or gather up all your food and move to the back of another line).

Need I go on? Life is full of little irritations. As someone has said, "It isn't the mountain ahead that wears you out, it's the grain of sand in your shoe." Put enough grains of sand together and they begin to feel like a mountain. Some burdens feel so heavy they almost seem impossible to bear. Live long enough, and you'll face a crushing crisis at work, a health problem an aspirin cannot fix, or a family problem you can no longer ignore. Even as you read this book, perhaps your faith is being tested by a lingering illness or an extended period of frustration as you try futilely to get a job, sell a house, resolve an interpersonal conflict, or lead a friend to the Lord.

> As someone has said, "It isn't the mountain ahead that wears you out, it's the grain of sand in your shoe."

The Bible doesn't say that trials are fun or easy to handle. It doesn't say to fake it and pretend everything's great. But it does tell us to persevere. It says, "Let us not become weary in doing good, for at the proper time we will reap a harvest if we do not give up" (Gal 6:9).

The Denver Broncos football team went to the Super Bowl in 1989, then fell to last place with a 5-11 record in 1990. Undeterred by their disappointing season and determined to do better the next year, some of the Broncos players wore T-shirts during their summer practices with "FIDO" printed on them. "FIDO" is short for "Forget It and Drive

An Unquenchable Determination to Persevere 10

On." The team's record improved dramatically to 12-4 in 1991, and by the end of the decade the Broncos won two consecutive Super Bowls. They had a bad year, but they managed to "forget it and drive on."

Jesus endured the cross for the "the joy set before him" (Heb 12:2). He saw that the outcome of his pain was going to be something good. Even amid persecution and trials of many kinds, we can develop spiritual staying power. We can persevere.

Trusting in God's Justice

But how does our suffering fit into God's big picture? If he loves us so much, is it fair that he allows us to endure so many heartaches? Believers have asked this question for centuries. What about the sufferings of Job, the martyrdom of Stephen, and Paul's thorn in the flesh?

The prophet Habakkuk complained, "How long, O Lord, must I call for help, but you do not listen? . . . Why do you make me look at injustice? Why do you tolerate wrong? Destruction and violence are before me; there is strife, and conflict abounds" (Hab 1:2,3).

In John's vision of Heaven, he saw "the souls of those who had been slain because of the word of God and the testimony they had maintained. They called out in a loud voice, 'How long, Sovereign Lord, holy and true, until you judge the inhabitants of the earth and avenge our blood?'" (Rev 6:9,10).

Suffering for their faith, the Thessalonians no doubt asked similar questions. So Paul urges them to trust in the justice of God. He assures them,

> All this is evidence that God's judgment is right, and as a result you will be counted worthy of the kingdom of God, for which you are suffering. God is just: He will pay back trouble to those who trouble you and give relief to you who are troubled, and to us as well. This will happen when the Lord Jesus is revealed from heaven in blazing fire with his powerful angels. He will punish those who do not know God and do not obey the gospel of our Lord Jesus. They will be punished with everlasting destruction and shut out from the presence of the Lord and from the majesty of his power on the day he comes to be glorified in his holy people and to be marveled at among all those who have believed. This includes you, because you believed our testimony to you (vv. 5-10).

There are several key points to notice in this Scripture text:

"God's judgment is right." He never makes a mistake. Life isn't fair, but God is. He is the perfect standard for what is right, the ultimate example of integrity. "Will not the Judge of all the earth do right?" (Gen 18:25).

"God is just." He will deal with every wrong, either by punishing it or by forgiving it. If someone causes trouble, God will "pay back trou-

ble" to him. If someone is doing what is right but suffering for it, God will "give relief" to him.

"This will happen when the Lord Jesus is revealed from heaven." Normally Paul has used the word "coming" (Greek *parousia*) to describe Jesus' return to earth (1 Thess 2:19; 3:13; 4:15; 5:23). Here he calls it the time when Jesus will be "revealed" (*apokalypsis*), emphasizing the uncovering of what has been hidden. When Jesus comes to judge the world, nothing will be hidden anymore. All will have to acknowledge his glory, even if they have previously refused to see the truth (Phil 2:10; Rev 1:7; 6:15-17). "The glory of the Lord will be revealed, and all mankind together will see it" (Isa 40:5).

"He will punish those who do not know God." Punishment is an uncomfortable thought, but it fits squarely with the idea of God's justice. Stuart Briscoe points out, "When the Bible says God exercises vengeance, it does not mean that he is into retaliation. It means he is committed to retribution. Retaliation is merely 'me getting even with you for what you did to me.' Retribution speaks of a rigorous system of justice."[3]

> "Retaliation is merely 'me getting even for what you did to me.' Retribution speaks of a rigorous system of justice."

"They will be punished with everlasting destruction and shut out from the presence of the Lord and from the majesty of his power." Scripture contains many solemn pronouncements about the eternal state of the wicked. Hell is described with vivid word-pictures like these:

- Fire of God's anger (Deut 32:22)
- Unquenchable flame (Mark 9:43-48)
- Fiery furnace (Matt 13:40-42)
- Lake of fire (Rev 20:14,15)
- Weeping and gnashing of teeth (Matt 13:42,50)
- Darkness (Matt 8:12; 22:13)
- Exclusion (Matt 25:41; Luke 13:23-28; Rev 22:14,15)
- Torment (Rev 14:10,11; Luke 16:23-28)
- Shame, everlasting contempt (Dan 12:1)
- Eternal judgment (Heb 6:2)
- Denial by the Lord (Matt 7:23; 10:33)
- Second death (Rev 2:11; 20:14; 21:8).

Nothing sounds worse, though, than the thought presented in 2 Thessalonians 1:9, which says the sinner will be "shut out from the presence of the Lord." The worst part of Hell will be missing out on the blessed presence of God. We were created to enjoy unbroken fellowship with our Creator, but sin separates us from him. Hell simply continues the breach already caused by sin.

The existence of Hell does not contradict the justice of God; it verifies and underscores the justice of God. John Stott explains:

. . . . [God's] wrath is evidence of his righteousness, and his anger against evil is evidence of his stand for what is good. How do I know that a person stands for what is good? One of the best ways is to see how angry he becomes about the opposite of good—evil. We live in a very tolerant society today. In many ways it is good to see this tolerance. But it is a pernicious thing in other ways. We are not to be so tolerant that we will put up with anything. That is spinelessness. We need to be courageous enough to stand up for the right in the face of wrong. Do we want God to reward righteousness? Do we want him to make good ultimately triumph? Then we have no alternative but to accept a God of judgment and anger—holy, righteous, and pure. He must visit his wrath and his anger on all who depart from him and all who insult his moral character.[4]

The good news is, there will also be great joy when Jesus "comes to be glorified in his holy people" and to "be marveled at among all those who have believed" (v. 10). We will stand in awe and amazement of him, marveling because at last we "see him as he is" (1 John 3:2). We need to persevere in our faith so we "will receive what he has promised" (Heb 10:26-36).

OBEYING THE GOOD NEWS

Second Thessalonians 1:8 warns about God's judgment upon those who "do not obey the gospel of our Lord Jesus." Usually we talk about "*believing* the gospel." What does it mean to "*obey*" it? Here's how James G. Van Buren explained this concept:

"I know a pair of grandparents who came up with an interesting idea. They wanted to leave some money for their grandchildren when they died. But since they were growing older and older, as were their grandchildren, they decided that the grandchildren should have the money earmarked for them now instead of after their death. They believed that these grandchildren, most of whom were married and rearing children, or in college, could better use this money now than at some future time.

"The immediate reception of the thousands of dollars was, of course, great news to the grandchildren. However, while the money was a 'free gift,' the gifts were in the form of checks. These had to be endorsed in order to make the money available to the grandchildren. Conditions had to be met, even though the money was a gift.

"We have 'good news' which tells us of Jesus' coming as our Redeemer, his life of goodness, his death on the cross, and his resurrection. This good news of salvation is a gift, 'not of works, lest any man should boast' (Eph 2:9).

"Yet this gospel must be 'obeyed,' as verse 8 of our printed text affirms. Christians proclaim 'good news,' but it not only must be heard, but also heeded. Confession of faith, baptism, and Christian living show one is 'obeying the gospel.'" (James G. Van Buren, *Adult Bible Teacher and Leader: Hope for the Future, 1, 2 Thessalonians; Revelation*, [Cincinnati: Standard Publishing, Spring, 1997] 253. Used by permission of the publisher.)

Living for the Glory of God

The good news is that God, by his grace, has made a way for our sins to be forgiven instead of punished. When we belong to Christ, we don't get what we deserve; we get something far better than our sins deserve. We are saved by grace (Eph 2:1-10, Titus 3:3-5).

Thus, Paul tells the Thessalonians, "With this in mind, we constantly pray for you, that our God may count you worthy of his calling, and that by his power he may fulfill every good purpose of yours and every act prompted by your faith" (v. 11). By our own human merit, we are not worthy of God's calling, but God's power does for us what we could never do for ourselves.

Did you ever walk on a moving sidewalk in a large airport terminal? Even though you still have to put forth your own effort, the moving sidewalk gives you the ability to move faster than you could walk on your own. When the Spirit of God is at work in our lives, we still have to put forth our own effort. We still have decisions to make and work to do, but God's Spirit provides the extra strength we need to persevere. A Yiddish proverb says, "God gives burdens, also shoulders."

A Yiddish proverb says, "God gives burdens, also shoulders."

Our motivation changes as well, for we don't need to do good works to impress others or to build ourselves up. In Christ we are motivated not by self-gratification but by faith in the Lord and a heart-felt desire to please him. Paul adds, "We pray this so that the name of our Lord Jesus may be glorified in you, and you in him, according to the grace of our God and the Lord Jesus Christ" (v. 12).

On the night before he died on the cross, Jesus "looked toward heaven and prayed: 'Father, the time has come. Glorify your Son, that your Son may glorify you" (John 17:1). In the Bible, "glory" often refers to the brightness, radiance, or splendor of a person, like the way a bride on her wedding day is radiant and glowing. Glory can refer to a person's fame or renown. To "glorify" others means to shine the spot-light on them so that they receive honor and so that others can see what they're really like. A Christian's goal is to glorify the Lord and shine the spotlight on him.

> **A Christian's goal is to glorify the Lord and shine the spotlight on him.**

To survive the ups and downs of the Christian life, we must devel-op an unquenchable determination to persevere. God will help us in the task. In the words of Victor Hugo, "Have courage for the great sorrows of life, and patience for the small ones. And when you have laborious-ly accomplished your daily task, go to sleep in peace. God is awake."

---

[1] Gary Weedman, *Philippians-Thessalonians* (Cincinnati: Standard, 1988) 202.

[2] Leon Morris, *The First and Second Epistles to the Thessalonians* (Grand Rapids: Eerdmans, 1959) 198.

[3] Stuart Briscoe, *Taking God Seriously* (Waco: Word, 1986) 112.

[4] Ibid., 114.

10 *An Unquenchable Determination to Persevere*

Developing Unquenchable Faith

1. What makes it hard for you to persevere in your faith as a Christian? What helps you to do so?

2. How often do you think about Hell? What do you think it will be like? (See Rev 20:11-15.)

3. How often do you think about Heaven? What do you think it will be like? (See Rev 21:1–22:5.)

4. *"The existence of Hell does not contradict the justice of God; it verifies and underscores the justice of God."* Do you agree or disagree with this statement? Explain.

5. How can you "shine the spotlight on the Lord" as a group? As an individual?

Memory Verse
2 Thess 1:11

With this in mind, we constantly pray for you, that our God may count you worthy of his calling, and that by his power he may fulfill every good purpose of yours and every act prompted by your faith.

CHAPTER ELEVEN

AN UNQUENCHABLE LOVE FOR THE TRUTH

2 THESSALONIANS 2:1-17; 3:1-5

God is always honest with us. He always tells the truth, even when the truth is hard for us to accept. God "does not lie" (Titus 1:2). In fact, "it is impossible for God to lie" (Heb 6:18). He is the foundation and the source of truth. There is nothing artificial, phony, or misleading about him. Jesus said, "If you hold to my teaching, you are really my disciples. Then you will know the truth, and the truth will set you free" (John 8:31,32).

By contrast, Satan is always dishonest. He constantly twists the truth, even when his words sound safe and compelling on the surface. Jesus said of the devil, "There is no truth in him. When he lies, he speaks his native language, for he is a liar and the father of lies" (John 8:44). In the Garden of Eden, Satan deceived Adam and Eve, and ever since he's been doing his best to create a deceptive environment where "evil men and impostors will go from bad to worse, deceiving and being deceived" (2 Tim 3:13).

God is always honest with us; Satan is always dishonest.

New Yorkers jokingly refer to the Long Island Expressway as "the world's biggest parking lot." This big wide road is regularly congested with six lanes of heavy traffic as commuters make their way into New York City day after day. When my family lived in New York, we noticed local residents referred to this highway by using its initials. Instead of the Long Island Expressway, they called it the "LIE." Jesus spoke of another big wide road many people travel, and it could also be called the "LIE," for it is a road based on Satan's misinformation. "Enter through the narrow gate," Jesus warned. "For wide is the gate and broad is the road that leads to destruction, and many enter through it. But small is the gate and narrow the road that leads to life, and only a few find it" (Matt 7:13,14).

In this kind of world, truth is a pearl of great price. It is a treasure to be sought, found, and carefully guarded. Proverbs 23:23 exhorts us to "buy the truth and do not sell it; get wisdom, discipline and understanding." The apostle John said, "It gave me great joy to have some brothers come and tell about your faithfulness to the truth and how you continue to walk in the truth" (3 John 3). Why was he so glad they were walking in the truth? Because "many deceivers . . . have gone out into the world" (2 John 7). Paul told Titus that an elder in the church "must hold firmly to the trustworthy message as it has been taught, so that he can encourage others by sound doctrine and refute those who oppose it" (Titus 1:9).

Recognizing the Counterfeit (2:1-12)

Satan's lies were threatening the Thessalonian church, so Paul warned them about some dangerous ideas they should not embrace.

Paul had a lot to say in his first epistle about "the coming of our Lord Jesus Christ and our being gathered to him" (v. 1). Evidently, though, some of the Thessalonian Christians had misconstrued his words.

Adding to their confusion, it appears that a report allegedly from Paul may have been circulating. Paul urges the Thessalonians "not to become easily unsettled or alarmed by some prophecy, report or letter supposed to have come from us" (v. 2). Paul tells them not to be "unsettled" (Greek *saleuo*, a word that appears in Acts 16:26, where an earthquake shook the prison). Nor does he want them to be "alarmed" (Greek *throeo*, which means to "frighten" or "trouble"—the same word Jesus used to warn the disciples not to be troubled about wars and rumors of wars in Matt 24:6).

What was this "prophecy, report or letter" supposedly from Paul? Some think it refers to a forged letter someone else wrote while claiming Paul was the author. (This could explain why Paul found it necessary to conclude this letter with his personal signature. See 2 Thess 3:17.) Others, though, think the problem was simply that the Thessalonians had misunderstood and misapplied Paul's message in 1 Thessalonians.

The apostle Peter warned about false teachers who deny that Jesus ever will come again at all (2 Pet 3:1-11). But the problem in Thessalonica was different. There, some were "saying that the day of the Lord has already come" (v. 2).

"Don't let anyone deceive you in any way" (v. 3). Paul goes on to mention two key events that must occur before the Lord's return. "That day will not come until the rebellion occurs and the man of lawlessness is revealed, the man doomed to destruction" (v. 3). First there must be a notable "rebellion" or apostasy, a great falling away from the truth of God. According to Wilbur Fields, the "falling away refers to that corruption of the apostles' teaching by heathenism which occurred during the early centuries of the church" and was propagated by the Roman Catholic church and by many Protestants as well.[1] Others think this unbounded burst of rebellion will occur at the end of time shortly before Christ returns. In either case, Paul is describing here the same kind of apostasy he details in 2 Timothy 3:1-5 where he says "there will be terrible times in the last days" (see also 1 Tim 4:1-3).

Also, Paul notes that before the return of Christ takes place, the "man of lawlessness" will be revealed. Who is this man? He is "lawless," which emphasizes the extent of the evil concentrated in him and "suggests his deliberate hostility to the known will of God."[2] He is "doomed to destruction," a phrase reminiscent of the ominous words Jesus applied to Judas the betrayer in John 6:70,71 and 17:12. Over the centuries believers have attempted to identify this man of lawlessness with various figures including Roman emperors, the popes, the beast of Revelation chapter 13, Adolf Hitler, the devil himself, or a future world ruler who gains political power and rules as the "antichrist." The spirit of "antichrist" is mentioned elsewhere in Scripture (1 John 2:18,22), and the Bible uses the word "antichrist" to mean anyone who denies Jesus is the Christ or that he came in the flesh (see 2 John 7). It's also clear from Scripture that "the spirit of the antichrist" was "already in the world" in the first century (1 John 4:3).

The man of lawlessness "is the secularist *par excellence*."

The man of lawlessness "is the secularist *par excellence*. The opposer and self-exalter is . . . a mocking parody of Christ."[3] "He will oppose and will exalt himself over everything that is called God or is worshiped, so that he sets himself up in God's temple" (v. 4). The church is God's temple (1 Cor 3:17, Eph 2:12), so this individual's wickedness is so great that he proclaims himself a religious leader with authority over God's people—even *"proclaiming himself to be God,"* which is utter

An Unquenchable Love for the Truth

blasphemy (v. 4). This evil one epitomizes "the pervasive power of evil in the world which ultimately derives from Satan himself."[4]

What else do we know about the man of lawlessness?

- At the time Paul wrote this letter, something or someone was "holding back" or restraining this evil one, but eventually the restraining power would be removed (vv. 6,7).
- "The secret power of lawlessness" that characterizes this individual was "already at work" in the first century when Paul wrote to the Thessalonians (v. 7).
- The lawless one tries to impress and deceive others with "counterfeit miracles, signs and wonders" (v. 9; see also 2 Cor 11:13-15).
- He will promote "every sort of evil that deceives those who are perishing" (v. 10).
- Ultimately the Lord Jesus will overthrow and destroy this evil one "by the splendor of his coming" (v. 8).

We struggle to understand what Paul is saying here, but the first-century Thessalonians had the advantage of hearing the apostle's explanation firsthand. "Don't you remember that when I was with you I used to tell you these things?" (v. 5). Paul had talked plainly about these matters when he visited Thessalonica earlier in his ministry. Perhaps it was easier for them to understand this difficult teaching than it is for us today.

Although many details in these verses are hard to fully explain, we cannot miss the main points Paul is making: (1) The coming of Jesus had not already occurred at the time when he wrote 2 Thessalonians, for some other events must take place first; (2) Satan is (and will continue to be) hard at work, attempting to thwart God's purposes; (3) Satan is a liar who uses "every sort of evil that deceives those who are perishing" (v. 10).

Those who willfully refuse "to love the truth and so be saved" (v. 10) have chosen their own fate. It's puzzling to read in verse 11, "For this reason God sends them a powerful delusion so that they will believe the lie." However, this verse should be understood along with Romans 1:18-32, where Paul teaches that when sinners persist in their rejection of the truth, eventually God "gives them over" to the sinful desires of their hearts and allows them to act out the shameful perversions they have chosen. The tragic result? "All will be condemned who have not believed the truth but have delighted in wickedness" (v. 12). These are sobering words, especially in our postmodern culture, which tends to downplay the seriousness of sin.

Professor Jon Weatherly summarizes this section as follows:

Paul regards the promised end-time to be already present because of the work of Christ. The prevalence of evil, variously manifested, is ultimately the work of Satan. That fact is already recognized by the Christians, but the world is unaware of it, having fallen prey to Satan's deceptive powers. But when Christ returns, he will reveal Satan and his activity for what it truly is, ending his rule over this age and consigning him to eternal punishment. Therefore, as long as evil still prevails in the world, the Christians can know that God's work is not yet complete. They can therefore be confident in the faithfulness and power of God, remaining true to the gospel despite the difficulties they face and looking forward to their vindication at the final judgment.[5]

We must believe the truth and reject the counterfeit. There's a lot at stake.

Holding onto the Genuine (2:13-17)

In the latter part of 2 Thessalonians chapter 2, however, Paul returns to a more encouraging tone. In sharp contrast to those who delight in wickedness and face condemnation for their sin, Paul was thankful for the believers in Thessalonica, his "brothers loved by the Lord" (v. 13).

"From the beginning," he says, "God chose you to be saved through the sanctifying work of the Spirit and through belief in the truth" (v. 13). Does this mean God arbitrarily chooses people for salvation? No, for this salvation still requires "belief in the truth" on the part of those who receive it. Personal faith is a necessary requirement for those who accept God's gracious gift (see John 1:12; 3:16; Heb 11:6). That's why Paul goes on to say, "He called you to this through our gospel, that you might share in the glory of our Lord Jesus Christ" (v. 14).

"Faith comes from hearing the message, and the message is heard through the word of Christ" (Rom 10:17). We must hold onto the genuine message God has given us in the New Testament. Paul says, "So then, brothers, stand firm and hold to the teachings we passed on to you, whether by word of mouth or by letter" (v. 15). Whether the inspired apostles preached orally or wrote with pen and ink, their words recorded in Scripture carried the full weight of the authority of Christ (see also 1 Cor 14:37; Eph 3:3-5; 1 Thess 2:13; 2 Pet 3:2).

We must believe the truth and reject the counterfeit.

How can we hold onto the truth of God? How can we keep from falling into deceptive, unbiblical teachings in our day? Here are two practical steps we can take:

1. *Prevent "truth decay" by grounding ourselves and our loved ones in the Word of God.* An old proverb says, "An ounce of prevention is worth a pound of cure." Someone else has said, "Better to build a fence by the edge of a cliff than a hospital at the bottom." The best way to prevent error is to teach truth. There's a great need today for preachers who will patiently, consistently preach through books of the Bible in an interesting, creative way. There's a great need for youth leaders and small group leaders who will resist the temptation to make their groups nothing but fun and games, and challenge their followers to go deeper in their knowledge of God. "Watch your life and doctrine closely. Persevere in them, because if you do, you will save both yourself and your hearers" (1 Tim 4:16).

The best way to prevent error is to teach truth.

2. *Get acquainted with the evidence that supports the reasonableness of Christian faith.* We need to know what we believe and why we believe it. First Peter 3:15 says, "But in your hearts set apart Christ as Lord. Always be prepared to give an answer to everyone who asks you to give the reason for the hope that you have. But do this with gentleness and respect." There are a number of quite readable books available today that can help us learn how to defend the Scriptures and the Christian worldview.[6]

God's truth is amazingly persuasive when it's heard and understood. *The Humanist* magazine advocates an atheistic, secular humanist point of view. One of the magazine's readers, however, wrote a letter to the editor and said he wanted to cancel his subscription. "During my subscription time," he wrote, "I couldn't help but notice that Christianity and the Bible were targets of criticism by the magazine. This negative attitude prompted me to investigate the subjects of criticism. I have now found the Lord and am a happy church member. Thank you for your help." *The Humanist* published the letter under a headline that said "Whoops"![7]

God's truth is amazingly persuasive when it's heard and understood.

Second Thessalonians chapter two closes with one of the most beautiful benedictions found anywhere in Scripture: "May our Lord Jesus Christ himself and God our Father, who loved us and by his grace gave us eternal encouragement and good hope, encourage your hearts and strengthen you in every good deed and word" (vv. 16,17).

Praying for Deliverance (3:1-5)

God doesn't tell us the truth so we can keep it to ourselves. Truth is meant to be humbly, patiently shared with others. Paul writes, "Finally, brothers, pray for us that the message of the Lord may spread rapidly and be honored, just as it was with you" (v. 1). This prayer was answered in New Testament times as the church experienced rapid growth (Acts 2:47; 9:31; 11:21,26). Can it happen today if we pray this same prayer? While we must wait patiently for God's Word to do its work, there are also times when "his Word runs swiftly" (Ps 147:15). Let's pray for the rapid advance of the gospel!

Truth is meant to be humbly, patiently shared with others.

Of course, Satan still does whatever he can to hinder the accurate and swift communication of the good news. So Paul urges, "And pray that we may be delivered from wicked and evil men, for not everyone has faith" (v. 2). F.F. Bruce notes, "By praying for the missionaries, the converts were participating in the spread of the gospel. The missionaries were much more concerned that their gospel witness should not be impeded than they were for their own safety; they were expendable 'earthen vessels' to which the treasure of the gospel was committed."[8] The early Christians showed similar boldness at other times when they faced persecution (Acts 4:29-31; 5:41,42).

Paul ends this section of his letter with some further words of encouragement and affirmation: "But the Lord is faithful, and he will strengthen and protect you from the evil one. We have confidence in the Lord that you are doing and will continue to do the things we command. May the Lord direct your hearts into God's love and Christ's perseverance" (vv. 4,5).

With that same confidence we can stand firm as well. We can develop an unquenchable commitment to God and his truth. We can "love our Lord Jesus Christ with an undying love" (Eph 6:24).

126

‡

C
H
A
P
T
E
R

[1] Wilbur Fields, *Thinking through Thessalonians* (Joplin, MO: College Press, 1963) 195.

[2] Ronald A. Ward, *Commentary on 1 & 2 Thessalonians* (Waco: Word, 1973) 155.

[3] Ibid., 156.

[4] Jon Weatherly, *1 & 2 Thessalonians* (Joplin, MO: College Press, 1996) 261.

[5] Ibid., 271.

[6] For example, Lee Strobel's *The Case for Christ* (Grand Rapids: Zondervan, 1998) and *The Case for Faith* (Grand Rapids: Zondervan, 2000). Also, my earlier book, *Taking Truth Next Door* (Cincinnati: Standard, 1999), contains small group guides to facilitate discussion of Christian evidences with believers and seekers.

[7] Calvin M. Osborne, "Whoops," *The Humanist* (November/December, 1993) 2.

[8] F.F. Bruce, *1 & 2 Thessalonians* (Waco: Word, 1982) 198, 199.

Developing Unquenchable Faith

1. Discuss some of the evidence you see that Satan is a deceiver. How is he twisting the truth in today's world? What are some of the lies he is getting people to believe?

2. What does it mean to "love the truth" (2 Thess 2:10)?

3. Do you believe that the world has become increasingly evil during your lifetime? Explain.

4. Read together 2 Thessalonians 3:3. How has God shown his faithfulness to you? How have you experienced his strength and protection?

5. Jesus said to pray that the heavenly Father will "lead us not into temptation, but deliver us from the evil one" (Matt 6:13). Close your group's time together by praying specifically for God's deliverance from the temptations you face.

| Memory Verse 2 Thess 2:15 | So then, brothers, stand firm and hold to the teachings we passed on to you, whether by word of mouth or by letter. |

CHAPTER TWELVE

AN UNQUENCHABLE COMMITMENT TO GOD'S WORK

2 THESSALONIANS 3:6-18

Someone has said, "If you want to put footprints in the sands of time, wear work-shoes." Another pundit points out, "The only place where success comes before work is in the dictionary."

Marie-Louise Febronie Meilleur was listed in the *Guinness Book of World Records* as the world's oldest person when she died in Ontario, Canada, at the age of 117. She believed that hard work was the secret to a long life. It's hard to argue with someone who lived that long!

There's nothing more practical than the Christian faith. It affects us right where we live on a daily basis—including the work we do. Even if you are an active church member, it's likely the 40 or 50 hours a week you spend at work far surpass the amount of time you spend at church.

> There's nothing more practical than the Christian faith.

What the Bible Says about Our Daily Work

Strangely enough, we do not hear many sermons about the way Christians should behave in the workplace. But this subject was very important to the apostle Paul; and in fact, the Bible has a lot to say about work.

Work Was Commanded and Honored in the Old Testament

Before Adam and Eve sinned, God told them to work and take care of the garden he had created (Gen 1:28; 2:15). Work wasn't a curse; in fact, even God himself worked for six days when he created the world (Gen 2:1-3). After sin entered the world, however, work lost some of its creativity and joy and became more frustrating and difficult (Gen 3:17-19).

In the Law of Moses, God commanded his people to observe a healthy balance of work and rest. "Six days you shall labor and do all your work," he said, but on the seventh day "you shall not do any work" (Exod 20:9,10; 23:12; 34:21). On the whole, the Hebrew people were industrious. First Kings chapters 4 through 9 describe how thousands of skilled workers built the temple in Solomon's day. According to Nehemiah 4:6, the Jews rebuilt the wall of Jerusalem quickly "for the people worked with all their heart."

Each Jewish father made it his goal to teach his son a trade. Some were farmers, carpenters, fishermen, stonecutters, shepherds, goldsmiths, tentmakers, perfume-makers, merchants, or blacksmiths. Jewish women were admired for their skills as well. The "noble wife" of Proverbs 31 cooked, bought real estate, planted a vineyard, made clothing, and served those in need.

Laziness was considered a serious sin. "Lazy hands make a man poor," wrote the wise man Solomon, "but diligent hands bring wealth" (Prov 10:4). "One who is slack in his work is brother to one who destroys," says Proverbs 18:9. A "sluggard" or a lazy individual brought dishonor to his family, and was the object of sarcastic humor (Prov 6:6-11; 10:4,5; 19:24; 24:30-34; 26:13-16). By itself, though, work could not bring fulfillment. With a melancholy tone, the book of Ecclesiastes asks, "What does a man get for all the toil and anxious striving with which he labors under the sun? All his days his work is pain and grief; even at night his mind does not rest. This too is meaningless." Nevertheless, "A man can do nothing better than to eat and drink and find satisfaction in his work. This too, I see, is from the hand of God" (Eccl 2:22-24).

Work Was Commanded and Honored in the New Testament

The New Testament has a lot to say about work as well. To illustrate his teachings, Jesus referred to people from many different walks of life: the homemaker who sweeps her house in search of a lost coin, the merchant who finds a choice pearl, the farmer who plants his seed in various kinds of soil, the soldier who obeys his commander's orders.

The book of Acts introduces us to a military officer named Cornelius (10:1), a leather-tanner named Simon (10:6), a dealer in purple cloth named Lydia (16:14), a prison guard whose family accepted Christ and were baptized in the middle of the night (16:23-36), and two tentmakers named Priscilla and Aquila (18:1-3).

Paul was a tentmaker. He taught that Christians not only earn money when we do an honest day's work; we also earn the respect of others, even those outside the Christian faith (1 Thess 4:11,12). He set a good example by working hard, night and day; and he was careful to avoid any impression that he was misusing his position as a preacher of the gospel to bilk people out of money (1 Cor 9:1-15; 1 Thess 2:9). Paul exhorted Timothy to work diligently in his role as an evangelist, and he urged that special honor should be given to elders who worked hard at their jobs (1 Tim 4:11-16; 5:17,18; 2 Tim 4:1-5). He gave specific guidance both to the "masters" who employed others and to the "slaves" who served them, and he summed up his instructions by saying to all, "Whatever you do, work at it with all your heart, as working for the Lord, not for men . . . . It is the Lord Christ you are serving" (Col 3:23,24).

The Sin of Idleness

All of this serves as background for Paul's concluding words in 2 Thessalonians chapter 3. Evidently some of the believers had become slack in their work. Perhaps they had adopted the view common in the Greek culture of the time that most work, especially manual labor, was undesirable and undignified. (Titus 1:12 quotes an ancient Cretan poet who described his own people as "lazy gluttons.") Some Bible students further conjecture that the Thessalonians had misunderstood Paul's teaching about the Lord's coming in 1 Thessalonians and concluded that, if Jesus was coming back soon, there was no reason to work at all.

Whatever the cause, the idleness of some of the members was having a negative effect on the church, and Paul considered this a serious issue. He wrote, "In the name of the Lord Jesus Christ, we command you, brothers, to keep away from every brother who is idle and does not live according to the teaching you received from us" (v. 6). In his previous letter, Paul told the church to "warn those who are idle" (1 Thess 5:14). This time he is more specific, for the situation appears to have worsened. If it sounds harsh to withdraw from the offender, remember: this is only to be done after someone demonstrates flagrant disregard for the teaching of the Lord. Even in such an extreme situation, Paul speaks of the offender as a "brother" in the Lord.

No one could call Paul a freeloader.

The Thessalonians were well acquainted with Paul's own work ethic. "For you yourselves know how you ought to follow our example. We were not idle when we were with you, nor did we eat anyone's food without paying for it. On the contrary, we worked night and day, laboring and toiling so that we would not be a burden to any of you" (vv. 7,8). No one could call Paul a freeloader. He worked both the day shift and the night shift, perhaps making tents to support himself as he did at Corinth, plus preaching and teaching on the side (Acts 17:2,3; 18:3,4). "We did this," he says, "not because we do not have the right to such help, but in order to make ourselves a model for you to follow" (v. 9).

It is right for someone who devotes a great deal of time to preaching and teaching the gospel to be paid for his work. Jesus said, "The worker deserves his wages" (Luke 10:7; see also 1 Cor 9:14 and Gal 6:6). However, it's also right for a servant of God to willingly forgo his privileges when doing so will further the Lord's work. Paul gave up the right to be paid for his preaching rather than appear self-serving.

> **God desires for all of us to experience
> the dignity and satisfaction of a good day's work.**

"For even when we were with you, we gave you this rule: 'If a man will not work, he shall not eat'" (v. 10). Wouldn't our nations and our families be blessed if everyone lived by this basic rule? God desires for all of us to experience the dignity and satisfaction of a good day's work. Work is good for our bodies, minds, and emotions. We appreciate our food more if we have worked to earn our daily bread. "The laborer's appetite works for him; his hunger drives him on" (Prov 16:26).

Of course, this rule does not mean withholding legitimate help from those who are unable to work. God's Word frequently tells us to meet the needs of the poor and those who cannot help themselves (Prov 22:9; Isa 58:7; 2 Cor 8:1-9). The early church provided generously for widows and orphans, and offered hospitality to travelers and missionaries who needed the church's support (Acts 4:32-34; 6:1-4; Phil 4:10-19; Heb 13:1,2; 3 John 5-8). It's wrong, however, to refuse to work when we have the opportunity to do so, and simply live off the generosity of others when we could be supporting ourselves. Those who are able must provide for our families (1 Tim 5:8) and provide for those in legitimate need (Eph 4:28).

131

> **God's Word frequently tells us to meet the needs of those
> who cannot help themselves; it's wrong, however,
> to refuse to work when we have the opportunity to do so.**

‡

C
H
A
P
T
E
R

An Unquenchable Commitment to God's Work 12

An old proverb reminds us that "an idle mind is the devil's workshop." Laziness and idleness breed other sins like gossip and self-centeredness. This was happening at Thessalonica, for Paul said, "We hear that some among you are idle. They are not busy; they are busybodies" (v. 11). The Lord wants his church to be a busy body, but he doesn't want us to be busybodies! At Timothy's church in Ephesus, young widows with too much time on their hands were falling prey to the same kind of temptation (see 1 Tim 5:13).

> The Lord wants his church to be a busy body,
> but he doesn't want us to be busybodies!

The solution is clear: "Such people we command and urge in the Lord Jesus Christ to settle down and earn the bread they eat" (v. 12).

The Hard Work of Church Discipline

"And as for you, brothers, never tire of doing what is right" (v. 13). The King James Version translates this verse, "But ye, brethren, be not weary in well-doing" (see also Gal 6:9). Life becomes tiresome for all of us at times. That's why we need an unquenchable commitment to carry out the Lord's work. "Well-doing" is more than merely the avoidance of wrongdoing. It's a positive lifestyle of service to God. Dorcas "was always doing good" (Acts 9:36), and Jesus "went about doing good" (Acts 10:38). We must never quit doing what is right.

Church discipline is one area where it's difficult to carry out God's work. How should we respond to another believer who is committing a flagrant, ongoing sin against God? Of course we should not be harsh or judgmental toward one another; yet should blatant sin in the body go unchallenged? Doesn't the Bible teach us to exhort and encourage one another, spurring one another on "toward love and good deeds" (Heb 10:24)? Paul considered the Thessalonians' idleness such a serious

132

‡

C
H
A
P
T
E
R

matter, he said in verse 14, "If anyone does not obey our instruction in this letter, take special note of him. Do not associate with him, in order that he may feel ashamed."

Discipline is an unpopular but important task in the church. Jesus laid down specific guidelines for dealing with a brother who falls into sin (Matt 18:15-17). When sexual immorality threatened the Corinthian church, it brought a firm response from the apostle Paul (1 Cor 5:1-13). In many situations where church discipline is called for, a brother or sister in Christ will respond well to a loving, one-on-one rebuke. "He who rebukes a man will in the end gain more favor than he who has a flattering tongue" (Prov 28:23).

In extreme cases, when the erring brother continues in a prolonged, unrepentant attitude of rebellion, stronger discipline is required. Paul told Titus, "Warn a divisive person once, and then warn him a second time. After that, have nothing to do with him. You may be sure that such a man is warped and sinful; he is self-condemned" (Titus 3:10,11).

Lest anyone would be too harsh, however, Paul added an important caution: "Yet do not regard him as an enemy, but warn him as a brother" (v. 15). Likewise, the Bible warns, "Brothers, if someone is caught in a sin, you who are spiritual should restore him gently. But watch yourself, or you also may be tempted" (Gal 6:1).

FURTHER THOUGHTS ON CHURCH DISCIPLINE

The Purposes of Church Discipline:

- *To uphold the authority of Christ.* Members of the body of Christ should not think we can insult God's holiness and live any way we want, while still enjoying all the privileges of the Christian life.
- *To maintain the purity of the church.* Even those outside the church take note of the way a congregation deals with sin in its midst (1 Cor 5:1). If allowed to go unchallenged and unchecked, sin corrupts and spreads (1 Cor 5:6,7).
- *To save the offender.* The goal is not to punish the straying brother, but to restore him so that his "spirit [will be] saved on the day of the Lord" (1 Cor 5:5).

The Practice of Church Discipline:

- *As private as possible.* Jesus said, "Go and show him his fault, just between the two of you. If he listens to you, you have won your brother over" (Matt 18:15).
- *As personal as possible.* Most discipline issues need to be handled with face-to-face discussions, certainly not through gossip or through impersonal policies handed down by boards or committees.

- *As prompt as possible.* Serious problems do not go away on their own. We must be careful not to overreact or act too hastily, but once we have all the facts and a confrontation is necessary, it's best not to put it off. If we can find the courage to deal with problems promptly, many times we can keep potentially bad situations from getting worse.
- *As prayerful as possible.* We need the strength and guidance of the Lord to "correct, rebuke and encourage—with great patience and careful instruction" (2 Tim 4:2).
- *As positive as possible.* Jesus couched his instructions about church discipline in the context of some other powerful teachings about humility, mercy, prayer, forgiveness, and concern for the lost (Matt 18:1-35). "No discipline seems pleasant at the time, but painful. Later on, however, it produces a harvest of righteousness and peace for those who have been trained by it" (Heb 12:11).

The Work of God in Us

Second Thessalonians closes on a positive note which emphasizes God's work, not ours. Paul prays, "Now may the Lord of peace himself give you peace at all times and in every way. The Lord be with you all" (v. 16).

Jesus promised to give his disciples peace that the world cannot give (John 14:27). Paul calls him the "Lord of peace" (v. 16)—an appropriate title since Jesus himself "is our peace" (Eph 2:14), the "Prince of Peace" (Isa 9:6). The Hebrews spoke of peace with the word *shalom*, an overall sense of well-being that comes from a right relationship with God. This peace, Paul notes, is available to us "at all times and in every way." Whenever we need it, we can find "the peace of God, which transcends all understanding" (Phil 4:7).

> The promise of God's presence is something we must never take for granted.

‡

C
H
A
P
T
E
R

Paul's blessing, "The Lord be with you all," may seem like a cliché. Yet, the promise of God's presence is something we must never take for granted. Because the Lord is always with us, we have the power to carry the gospel to the ends of the earth (Matt 28:20; Acts 1:8). Because the Lord is with us, we can find contentment in all sorts of circumstances (Phil 4:11-13; Heb 13:5,6). Because the Lord is with us, we can even face death with peace and hope (2 Cor 5:7-9; Phil 1:20-25).

William Arthur Ward said, "God's strength behind you, his concern for you, his love within you, and his arms beneath you are more than sufficient for the job ahead of you."[1]

Verse 17 contains a handwritten salutation from the apostle: "I, Paul, write this greeting in my own hand, which is the distinguishing mark in all my letters. This is how I write" (v. 17). Why did Paul find it necessary to call attention to his signature? Perhaps he did so to highlight his personal concern for the Thessalonians. Penning this letter was not an impersonal exercise for Paul. He cared about his readers like a shepherd cares for his sheep, and he wanted them to know that this letter came from his heart. However, the main reason Paul signed this letter so prominently was probably because rumors were circulating about other letters supposedly from him (2 Thess 2:2). Paul wanted his friends to distinguish his authentic letters from the counterfeits. (See also Gal 6:11.)

It's fitting that Paul ends this letter by saying, "The grace of our Lord Jesus Christ be with you all" (v. 18). God's grace was one of the great themes of Paul's ministry and a dominant force of his life. He was so motivated by grace, so captivated by the gospel, he told the Ephesian elders, "I consider my life worth nothing to me, if only I may finish the race and complete the task the Lord Jesus has given me—the task of testifying to the gospel of God's grace" (Acts 20:24).

Paul had an unquenchable faith—a blazing passion to love and serve the Lord. By God's grace, we can live our lives that way too.

Let's keep fanning the flame.

---

[1] Cited by James G. Van Buren, *Hope for the Future: 1 & 2 Thessalonians, Revelation* (Cincinnati: Standard Publishing, 1997) 261.

Developing Unquenchable Faith

1. Do you consider yourself a hard worker? Most of the time, do you find your daily work enjoyable? Why, or why not?

2. How do you serve God in your daily work? Is it easy for you to see the connection between your faith in the Lord and what you do for a living? Why, or why not?

3. How might today's world be different if most people put into practice the Bible's instructions in 2 Thessalonians 3:6-13?

4. Have you ever been involved in a situation where church discipline has been applied? What were the results? What did you learn from the experience?

5. Spend a few minutes in your group reflecting on what you have learned from your study of 1 and 2 Thessalonians.

   • What are the most memorable lessons you have learned from these two books of the Bible?

   • How has the Lord spoken to you individually, and to your group, during these studies? Are you doing anything differently because of what you have learned?

6. Close the group with prayer, and read together Paul's closing blessings in 2 Thessalonians 3:16 and 3:18.

Memory Verse
2 Thess 3:16

Now may the Lord of peace himself give you peace at all times and in every way. The Lord be with all of you.

About the Author

After years of ministry with growing churches in New York, Ohio, and Indiana, David Faust now serves as president of Cincinnati Bible College & Seminary in Cincinnati, Ohio, and Executive Editor of *The Lookout* magazine. He's the author of several books, including *Faith under Fire*, *Married for Good*, and *Taking Truth Next Door*.

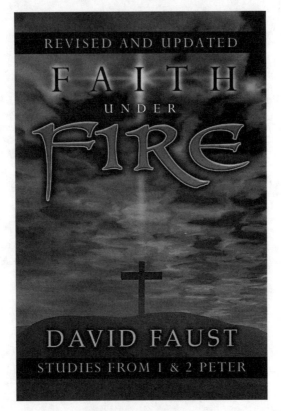

Married for Good

David Faust

Marriage is often portrayed by TV sitcoms, talk shows, and the popular magazines as something you endure rather than enjoy. But the opposite is true if couples prepare themselves before "the honeymoon is over." In his book, *Married for Good*, David Faust with humor and clever insight provides 31 observations for couples to T.A.L.K. through. This provides a valuable and rewarding experience that opens the door of communication and provides tools that will benefit couples of any age and any stage of marriage.

128 pages, hardbound, SC-911-5, $11.99

1-800-289-3300 • www.heartspringpublishing.com

THESSALONIANS MEMORY VERSES

Cut on dotted line

1 Thessalonians 1:3
"We continually remember before our God and Father your work produced by faith, your labor prompted by love, and your endurance inspired by hope in our Lord Jesus Christ."

1 Thessalonians 1:8
"The Lord's message rang out from you . . . your faith in God has become known everywhere."

1 Thessalonians 2:11,12
"For you know that we dealt with each of you as a father deals with his own children, 12encouraging, comforting and urging you to live lives worthy of God, who calls you into his kingdom and glory."

1 Thessalonians 2:13
"And we also thank God continually because, when you received the word of God, which you heard from us, you accepted it not as the word of men, but as it actually is, the word of God, which is at work in you who believe."

1 Thessalonians 2:19,20
"For what is our hope, our joy, or the crown in which we will glory in the presence of our Lord Jesus when he comes? Is it not you? 20Indeed, you are our glory and joy."

1 Thessalonians 4:3,4
"It is God's will that you should be holy; that you should avoid sexual immorality; 4that each of you should learn to control his own body in a way that is holy and honorable."

1 Thessalonians 4:16
"For the Lord himself will come down from heaven, with a loud command, with the voice of the archangel and with the trumpet call of God, and the dead in Christ will rise first."

1 Thessalonians 5:5,6
"You are all sons of the light and sons of the day. We do not belong to the night or to the darkness. 6So then, let us not be like others, who are asleep, but let us be alert and self-controlled."

1 Thessalonians 5:11
"Therefore encourage one another and build each other up, just as in fact you are doing."

2 Thessalonians 1:11
"With this in mind, we constantly pray for you, that our God may count you worthy of his calling, and that by his power he may fulfill every good purpose of yours and every act prompted by your faith."

2 Thessalonians 2:15
"So then, brothers, stand firm and hold to the teachings we passed on to you, whether by word of mouth or by letter."

2 Thessalonians 3:16
"Now may the Lord of peace himself give you peace at all times and in every way. The Lord be with all of you."

HEART
SPRING
JOPLIN, MISSOURI · 1.800.289.3300
WWW.HEARTSPRINGPUBLISHING.COM